Thou Shall Not Suffer

Thou Shall
Not Suffer

7 STEPS
to a Life *of* JOY

Mark Anthony Lord

Hierophantpublishing

Cover design by Adrian Morgan
Cover art by Birkenheuer Photography
Interior design by Jane Hagaman

Hierophant Publishing
8301 Broadway, Suite 219
San Antonio, TX 78209
888-800-4240
www.hierophantpublishing.com

If you are unable to order this book from your local bookseller,
you may order directly from the publisher.

Library of Congress Control Number: 2013954399

ISBN 978-1-938289-19-4

10 9 8 7 6 5 4 3 2 1

Printed on acid-free paper in the United States of America

To Patrick

Suffering

A man, how he suffered, though his life was so great.

He never could see, till he arrived at the pearly gates.

To get into heaven, which is what he wanted to do,

An Angel said, "Man, you must do a past life review."

The man turned around as he saw his whole life,

All the ways that he struggled and filled it with strife.

Most of his problems, 99 percent or more,

Were caused by his choices to blame and keep score.

His suffering was not as he thought all along,

That he deserved it because he was inherently wrong.

He watched in amazement as his troubles became clear,

Most often instead of love, he chose anger, and fear.

He saw he had power at every moment to be free,

To be happy, contented, to let God take the lead.

Then suddenly he laughed until he dropped to his knees,

As he realized all the suffering was just a bad dream.

Contents

Introduction   ix

Chapter 1   1
    Get a New God

Chapter 2   21
    Forgive Yourself and Others

Chapter 3   37
    Love Yourself Madly

Chapter 4   57
    Want What You Want

Chapter 5   75
    Surrender

Chapter 6   93
    Generously Receive

Chapter 7   107
    Give Yourself Away

Conclusion   119

Acknowledgments   123

Introduction

As the founder and senior minister of the Bodhi Spiritual Center in Chicago, I have taught spirituality to thousands of people. I often speak about the new era that we are now in, and one of the major changes required for all of us to really awaken to a greater freedom and joy—the end of personal suffering. I passionately tell them about a world of ease and grace and how, as the Bible says, the Kingdom of Heaven is at hand—right here and all around us. I tell them that not only are we here to be happy, prosperous, and free, but that it is our responsibility, our part of healing the world.

Somewhere between ease and grace and healing the world I begin to lose a lot of people to the chattering of their own mind saying, "This cannot be true. It can't be that easy." And that's when they start to push back and argue for their limitations. "Suffering is inevitable," they tell me; it's necessary. I am told there is no way around it. Suffering is a part of being human.

I am certain we are not here to be depressed, disappointed, or discouraged about life. We weren't born to waste our time worrying and fretting, pining for love and attention, and feeling unfulfilled. I am absolutely positive we are not here to suffer.

I do not deny that suffering is happening. We've all faced hard times: the loss of a job, illness, financial troubles, relationship difficulties, divorce, death, or addiction. But what if there were a way to face the inevitable and often unexpected challenges of life without having to suffer? What if it were possible to experience all the trials life may bring from a place of acceptance, curiosity, strength, and a spiritual perspective that allows you to remain connected to your joy and appreciation throughout it all?

I believe this is not only possible, it is actually the way we are meant to live. This is what I call the Kingdom of Heaven. It is not a place but a state of mind, an inner reality and point of focus that remains calm and connected to the spirit of love and oneness during the storms of life that come and go. This Kingdom of God is always right here, right now. It has no specific geographical location, but instead is perfectly located within you. It is everywhere you go and in every situation you find yourself.

I didn't always think this way. I spent many years suffering, not so much from the circumstances of my life, which at times were very hard, but from my inability to handle them. I didn't know there was another way to think, feel, or respond. I didn't know how to care for myself when I needed it most. I would say that at that time life was happening to me. And I was doing what I saw most everyone around me doing—complaining, commiserating, and blaming others.

My journey to become free began when I was in my twenties. I was fresh out of college and living in the big city. I felt very alone and afraid. Lofty dreams combined with low self-esteem caused me to create false, confident personas to cover up my sense of unworthiness. I desperately needed everyone to like me. I was obsessed to impress, which meant I overspent and undernourished myself. I didn't give myself enough food, self-care, or self-affirmation, while I indulged in storytelling and escaped my painful reality with all kinds of vapid distractions.

I was not happy, and in fact I was pretty darn depressed. Believe me, I really wanted a great life, just as I imagine you do. I wanted to feel good inside and to experience accomplishment and fulfillment. I wanted a loving, life-long relationship; meaningful friendships; love and laughter. I wanted the best that life could offer, but I didn't know how to get it, and the tools I had been given as a child were not working. The tools I was using perpetuated the story of myself as a victim to the world, unable to really be happy and free, and kept me on the never-ending cycle of suffering.

As I started to wake up to the many ways I was suffering in life, I also started to see how pervasive this suffering thing was. Everybody was doing it! In ways large and small my family, friends, neighbors, community, school, government, and church were all engaged in the suffering game. There was a worldwide suffering epidemic, and very few were getting the medicine they needed to break free. The good news, if there was any to be found, was that I wasn't alone in this suffering game. The bad news was that I *felt* alone, with no idea how to find my way out.

I was sharing my story of woe with a friend, who loved me but was done hearing about it, and she handed me what looked like a business card that had this Bible quote on it—Romans 12:2: "And do not be conformed to this world, but be transformed by the renewing of your mind, in order to prove by you what is that good and pleasing and perfect will of God."

I put the card in my pocket without much consideration, but later that night I pulled it out and reread it. Was I conformed to this world? What the heck did that mean? As I contemplated this, I realized that I did care too much about what the world thought. I almost always compared myself to others and from that comparison decided whether I was one up or one down. I made many of my choices—where to eat, what to wear, who I did or didn't become friends with, how I spent my time, and what I chose to do for my career—based on what the media said was in or out, as well as what everybody else thought about it. I lived to please others, and I thought I was happy only if you liked me.

I felt overly responsible for the people around me. I cared far too much about what I thought my family thought about the way I was choosing to live my life. When the world cried poor, I was poor. When the world did well, I did well. I rode the waves not even knowing there was another option. Suddenly I became powerfully sober to the fact that I was 100 percent conformed to this world.

I intuitively knew not to be too hard on myself. Life as we know it, and as the world is recreating over and over, *is* suffering because it is socially acceptable, supported, and even expected that we conform; we are taught from before we can walk and talk to deny our true self. We are encouraged to put ourselves last on the list, to do what others want us to do to make them happy, and if we don't then we are labeled selfish.

For those who are committed to following the rules of this world at the expense of denying their truth, living for other people instead of themselves, feeling shame about their passions and wanting, all in order to belong—life is suffering. For those who are asleep to the fact that they actually have a choice and are free to radically love themselves with all their strengths and weaknesses, fantasies and foibles, hopes and desires—life is suffering. For all those who are silent or who lie because they are afraid to tell their truth for fear of rejection or abandonment, ridicule or embarrassment—life is suffering.

I discovered the real problem was my mind! Behind all the behavioral choices I was making was this mind that kept telling me lies about how awful and bad I was. Where did those voices come from? And how the heck was I going to shut them off? Clearly the mind had to be renewed.

Although new to me, this revelation was made centuries ago. Sitting under the Bodhi tree in deep meditation, the Buddha awoke to the fact that "life is suffering." He realized that the world was a reflection of his thoughts. What he feared and judged was actually what he was seeing and experiencing in his day-to-day life. He realized that the mind was making up stories that he believed without question. This caused him to become emotionally activated, which was the core of his suffering.

Even more fantastic, the Buddha discovered it wasn't his individual mind that was thinking the guilt-ridden, judgmental, self-sabotaging thoughts. When he awakened he instantly became the observer of the *one* mind that everyone shared. He recognized that the thoughts of the mind weren't even personal, though they appeared to be. As he became able to observe his thoughts without becoming attached to them he became "peaceful beyond all human understanding." He was renewed. He awakened, which meant he was no longer a slave to the thoughts but the master, and in his mastery he transcended suffering.

The second half of the Bible quote my friend gave me is what really rocked my world. I was being told to "prove what was the good and pleasing and perfect will of God." Me? I'm to prove the will of God?

Bam! I suddenly realized the real problem was that I really didn't know what the perfect will of God was. From as far back as I could remember the will of God was to suffer. Heck, that's what he made his son do, right?

Burned in my memory is an image of me as a seven-year-old boy, sitting with my family in a pew at Mass. The priest was speaking, but I wasn't listening. I was staring up at an enormous statue of Jesus on the cross. His head, which was hanging down to the right, had a crown of thorns on it. Blood was trickling down his face. Nails were holding him to the cross by the wrists and feet. He was clearly in pain. He was sad, broken, betrayed, and. . . suffering, big time! I mean really, really suffering. And for whom? Me! He died for my sins. Oh dear God, I didn't even know what the heck I'd done to make him have to die, but it obviously was bad.

Something was really wrong with this picture of a suffering savior who just hung there week after week, year after year, for centuries transmitting the same message over and over: I died for you. You need to feel guilty, but also be grateful. Feel ashamed, but be sure to love me.

How confusing. After all he did for the world and me, surely I had no right to not suffer.

I was told that it was God's will that I suffer here on earth and that I would be rewarded for it later. Doing without, sacrificing my own wants would make God happy. Putting others' needs before my own was the right way to be. I got the message that if I did these things, when I died God would be pleased (if he'd pardon my cheating on my SAT test, my sexual desires, and a few thousand other things). Then I could finally be free of suffering. But not until then.

That's intense and violent imagery for an adult to handle, not to mention a young child. The God I learned about was mean! M-E-A-N. Who wants to turn to him and figure out his will? I was too busy running away from him, trying my best to hide my secret shame and desires.

Today I feel so blessed, because when it comes to God my mind has been renewed. Not only do I no longer believe God is mean, I experience God as an infinite, unlimited goodness that is always available. Right now. Not after you lose that weight or stop doing that thing you're ashamed of. Not once you have more money or start volunteering. God's goodness is absolute, which means it is perfect and has nothing to do with time, space, or circumstance. I also experience God as deeply personal—within me as a beloved, nonjudgmental best friend. It took a lot of years and perseverance to surrender the old ideas and to have my mind renewed, and even more to start living and accepting it as my truth and experience of life. But I am certain that this is possible for you, too.

What Suffering Is Not

It's important for us to discern between what is and is not suffering. Freedom from suffering does not mean that there will never be any pain or sorrow, that you'll never have to exert yourself or work hard, and that you get to be happy 24/7/365.

Back in the early nineties, a spiritual teacher I respected said, "I am *always* happy. I am never sad or depressed." I was younger and hopeful and so I made that my goal. But as I matured in my spirituality I realized that just wasn't realistic. I did feel sad and even depressed at times. I did feel confused and afraid. I felt pain at times, be it physical or emotional. To feel pain, grief, sadness, or anger is actually not suffering. Feelings are natural. They help us heal and move forward.

There are countless ways in which you, I, and everyone else repress, ignore, judge, and shame the feelings we don't want others to see for fear of ridicule and rejection. The bottom line is that our culture is not designed to honor and support people in having their feelings. Feelings can be unattractive, complicated, and messy. I get it. But, I'm no longer willing to wait for the world to say it's OK for me to have all my feelings so I can be authentic and healthy. I suggest you not wait either.

What I know is that you don't need to be happy all the time. What's more important is that you be authentic and available to your darker feelings like sadness, grief, fear, embarrassment, anger, jealousy, envy, etc. They are your messengers. They get ignited as a signal that tells you when you are off course, when you are doing or thinking something that isn't for your highest good. These feelings, when they are experienced fully, free of shame or guilt, can be acknowledged, owned, welcomed, and more easily moved through.

What Suffering Is

Suffering has billions of people trapped in its grip, seduced by its stories and convinced that it is the right way to go. Suffering is interwoven into the fabric of our societies, religions, education, government, and legal systems. It is deeply rooted within our families and relationships.

Suffering is an internal experience of self-rejection, self-denial, self-hatred, self-repression, self-punishment, and the recycling of negative thoughts and beliefs that cause unnecessary, present-moment shame, blame, guilt, and agony. What's the common denominator here? Your self. Suffering is experienced in you—not outside. Suffering is the prolonged denial, repression, projection, and exaggeration of any dark feelings. It is remaining stuck in an emotion past its usefulness and rightful ending.

Suffering is . . .

> Believing you are separate from an uncondi-
  tionally loving, generous, totally-for-you God.
> Believing and personalizing the negative chatter
  of the mind.
> Regretting, not forgiving, and therefore living
  in the past.
> Putting your own goals, needs, and self-care last.
> Trying to control anything other than you, such
  as people, places, and things.
> Blocking life's generous solutions and assistance
  by not allowing yourself to receive help, care,
  nurturance, love, and support.
> Being stingy with your God-given gifts and
  talents that could help others prosper and be
  happy.

Eckhart Tolle said, "Suffering is necessary until you realize it is unnecessary." To me, what he is saying is that suffering is a path to awakening, albeit a painful and sometimes
long one. Once you see there is an easier and gentler way,
then you no longer need pain to push you. Suddenly you
experience being pulled by inspiration, by vision and possibility. You no longer need suffering to tell you something
is off because you're focused on following what feels good
and true to you. This is when you have crossed the thresh-
old into a new way of thinking and being where suffering
is unnecessary—a waste of time and energy.

Ultimately suffering is a dream of separation from the Divine, Infinite Love, Source, God (whatever name you choose). The dream of being separate from God is not true; it cannot and never will be. Once you awaken from this nightmare, you will know this and it will feel so right to you. But until then, well, we've got some work to do.

The New Era Is Now

The truth is you cannot awaken to your innate freedom and joy while continuing to carry your tired, suffering baggage. It is ours to shed, and the great news is that discarding the burden is easier than ever before. Years ago we would have heard, "Who are you to think yourself so above it all?" Not that we won't ever hear this voice along our path to freedom, or other resistant stances from within and from others, but today it is much easier to embrace the idea that we all are above the energy, the story, and the need to suffer.

We are now living in the new era, one where more and more people are describing themselves as spiritual and aware of a connectivity between all life that is to be nurtured. Children are coming into the world freer to be themselves. From books to billboards, messages of possibility, healing, and encouragement to live your dreams are everywhere. And most importantly, in the new era suffering is no longer required.

This is great news. But the shift needed for all of humanity to awaken into greater cooperation, care, and support for ourselves, each other, and all of life will not come in one fell swoop. Instead, each person will be individually invited to step off the wheel of suffering. I truly believe there will come a time when we reach a tipping point at which it will be exponentially easier for groups of people to surrender suffering. But for today, the world needs those individuals who are willing to wake up from their personal story of suffering. Are you one of those people? Are you ready and willing to join me in ending suffering on this planet?

"Really? Me? The world needs little ole me?" you ask. *Yes. Desperately!* Just breathe that in for a moment. We have been conditioned to believe we don't matter, or that the problem is too big so there's nothing we can do, when in fact it's exactly the opposite. All you do for yourself in the name of freedom blesses everyone and ultimately changes the entire fabric of humanity, of which you are an integral part.

I am certain the world will benefit, and benefit greatly, from your commitment to end your suffering. But let's be clear; first and foremost, this freedom is for you. This Universe adores you and wants you to know and experience its power, joy, and infinite goodness. Inherent within you is the ability to change every negative perception and false belief. Within you there is enough genius and creativity to solve every existing problem—especially the age-old agreement that we must suffer. It is time for this truth to be more than a nice idea. It is time for it to be made manifest and experienced in your life.

I know it is possible to be free of suffering because I have experienced it. I've walked the path to my own liberation, and what I have discovered is that it's not about intellectually understanding the details and subtleties of your suffering. Understanding alone avails us of nothing. It is instead about focusing your time and attention on self-care, self-acceptance, self-appreciation, and in letting go and allowing the God of your being to prove His/Her/Its "good, pleasing, and perfect will" for you.

The first step in ending your suffering is to uncover and discard all negative concepts projected upon the God of your being. What I know is that God's perfect will is literally right within you. You're wired to know it, feel it, and live it. But I'm guessing you, like me, were told some pretty scary stuff that may be keeping you from really trusting God. We need to get all that gunk and junk out of the way.

Oh, the peace and happiness you will feel when you allow yourself to become fully released from any and all false beliefs about God! I just can't wait. Let's get started now.

1

Get a New God

I believe in God, but not as one thing, not as an old man in the sky. I believe that what people call God is something in all of us. I believe that what Jesus and Mohammed and Buddha and all the rest said was right. It's just that the translations have gone wrong.

—John Lennon

Imagine a three-year-old boy riding a tricycle, happy and free as he whips down the sidewalk. Now see that same boy at age seven. He is bigger and stronger but still riding that same tricycle. He looks awkward and uncomfortable, all knees and elbows jutting out as he pedals along, but he hasn't completely outgrown the trike yet so he can still get around. Now see him at age fourteen. He is much too big for the tricycle but is still riding it. He actually looks ridiculous but insists this is the bike for him. Let's go for one more. The boy, who is now a thirty-two-year-old man, is *still* riding his tricycle. At this point you would easily consider him certifiably crazy.

I have discovered that many people are like this man and his tricycle when it comes to their relationship with God. They cling to their childish ideas and concepts even though they have long outgrown them. They remain attached to the fairy tales of an external God, which are clearly no longer working for them in adulthood. Or they realize it's ludicrous to try and keep this storybook God alive, but because they have no alternative they throw God out altogether.

While I was in ministerial school in Los Angeles I worked part time as a spiritual counselor at a 12-step recovery center. I met many different kinds of people there, from doctors to priests, homemakers to well-known entertainers. Addiction is a spiritual disease, which requires a spiritual solution. My job was to help them heal their relationship with God so they had a fighting chance of recovering.

Many patients whom I worked with were acutely conflicted. I would often hear them say, "I do believe God is loving, but I'm also afraid that I might displease or anger him." More often than not they experienced God as punishing or nowhere to be found. Really, the God of their understanding was an exaggerated version of the world that told them they were losers, deeply flawed, and that if they would just try harder they could stop their addictive behaviors. Most prayed God would free them of their addictions more times than they could count, but the God they were praying to was their childhood under-standing—the one they thought didn't love or care for them. In desperation they turned to their tricycle God who clearly didn't work.

You don't need to be an addict to have a messed up idea about God. I've come to discover that most everyone I teach could use some healing in this area. When I work with my newer students I begin by asking them to tell me every negative thing they've thought, learned, or heard about God. Not everybody has exactly the same ideas, of course, but there are common themes.

God tends to be male, domineering, and able to watch our every move from someplace "on high." Some were told his job is to welcome the good people into heaven and send the bad people to hell to burn for eternity. He keeps score, though whether he answers people's prayers or not seems arbitrary, leaving many feeling abandoned and confused. He has a lot of rules on how we are and aren't supposed to behave. He wants us to ignore our inherent desires, especially the sexual ones. If you were raised Christian, you were most likely told that you had to accept Jesus as your personal savior and that those who didn't were out of luck—to hell they went. It seemed clear that God had favorites, but who were they? And how did you really know if you were one of them?

It's a sobering moment when we see how easily these negative, fearful ideas about God can be accessed with just a bit of coaxing. Even though you and I have long outgrown many of these childhood images, they still remain in us, especially when we feel afraid, alone, and in need of deep healing and comfort. It is during these times when our understanding of God either serves and carries us through or leaves us feeling even more alone and afraid.

The Bible says, "You cannot serve two masters." You can't believe in an unconditionally loving God and a punishing God at the same time; but many people pretend they can.

There's a problem with having that old, punishing God still living inside you, even if you declare it a distant, rejected memory. When you encounter challenging times in your life—when you feel up against the wall —that God surfaces as a victimizer. Instead of turning to God for hope and inspiration when you need them most, there you are feeling alone and unsupported. Even those of you who have many good feelings about God can find yourself in hard times and wondering, "Why is this happening to me? What did I do to deserve this?"

With the industrial revolution came so many advancements and comforts. Modern life has met and exceeded our physical needs. But as our physical comforts have increased, all around us we see people in the throes of depression, loneliness, and a sense of "what's it all for?" This is called existential suffering. It is painful and scary.

In this world of plenty, many people today are walking around obsessed with their problems. We struggle with neurosis, insecurity, intimacy issues, money troubles, fears, and soft or hard addictions. Some of us feel like crap on the inside, unworthy and not good enough. This is our collective soul crying out for its spiritual evolution and sense of meaning. Our spiritual advancement has not kept pace with our technical advancement, to say the least. It's time to "catch up" spiritually. It is time to get back to God. But I am not talking about the tricycle God. We've got to get a new one—a more mature, two-wheeling God that works for us in every way.

What if that scary, vengeful God were just made up? What if you and I have been force-fed a bad fairy tale about God? This monster of an idea got a hold of us way before we were ever close to being capable of reasoning or choosing otherwise. I was given no other option, so I took it all—hook, line, and sinker. The great news is that if we made this God up then we can unmake this image; blow it up and create a brand-new, more expansive one.

Right now, you can become liberated and create a personal, truly unconditionally loving God—one that works through you and for you. I know this may sound like a crazy concept, but it's true. You create God all the time, so let's create one that works.

Fire the Old God

If you were going to rehab an old, dilapidated house, the first thing you would need to do is clear out all the debris and garbage that's in the way. From there you could begin deciding what to keep, what needs to be restored, and what needs to be thrown out. Imagine for a moment that you have all the finances, time, and energy that you need to rehab this home. You have a team of the best architects, contractors, and builders that can be found. I invite you to feel as excited about clearing out the old God and getting a new one as you would if you really were building the house of your dreams.

I created an exercise many years ago where I ask people to write a termination letter informing the old God he is no longer needed. He has served his time, but the job is over. This can be a fun exercise as well as deeply meaningful and transformational.

Here's an example:

Dear Old God,

Effective immediately your services are no longer required. I have spent way too many years under your punishing and shaming control, and it is over! You were never there for me when I was a kid and needed you. I felt so deeply afraid of you and your judgment. You never comforted me or made me feel good about myself. You did a really bad job of helping me feel and see you. I've never felt loved by you; instead, I mostly felt not good enough and like I had to continually jump through hoops to get your attention and make you happy. I never could be good enough, and I am done trying. I am done feeling unworthy and afraid around you. You are a delusional, needy, scary, unforgiving, unavailable God who no longer gets to have residence in my mind, body, spirit, and life. It is time for me to become free of you and time for you to be on your way. Your termination is effective immediately. There will be no severance pay and no opportunity for you to return. This charade is over, and you are out!

Not sincerely,

Mark Anthony

Surprisingly, when I have students read the letters they have written out loud their classmates find themselves laughing. Why? It can be painful, but often it is humorous to realize that when it comes to God, they've been riding a tricycle for far too long and they can do something about it.

As you can see, it's important to be strong; not to take it out on God, but to get in touch with any anger or resentment that may be lying dormant. It's important and powerful to use your voice to set yourself free. This exercise is simple, but it can also be deeply transformational if you will let it. I've had some people write pages, leaving no stone unturned in order to set themselves free.

I encourage you to tell God what didn't work for you and how you may have felt abandoned, judged, afraid, or alone. Get as specific as you need to, and don't hold back. This is your opportunity to get it all out.

Be sure to take all the time you need to write your termination letter. Even if you don't perceive this being a big issue for you, I ask that you go as deeply into your psyche as you can to detox yourself of any and every negative, separating idea of God that is in there. Be specific. If your parents divorced and God was not there for you or did not bring them back together like you wanted, then write that down. If you were abused or neglected, put that in there too. The point of this exercise is to allow the young, unenlightened part of you to have a say.

After you have completed your letter I encourage you to seek out a trusted friend, therapist, sponsor, or beloved family member to share it with. Part of the healing process is to be seen and witnessed. Ask this person to listen with their hearts and to be a space of total acceptance of your freedom. I'm certain the work you've done will bless and set him or her free, too.

Remember, before you can build your expansive, beautiful new home in which you will live safely and happily, you need to get all the junk out.

Create a New God

Once we have terminated the old God, our next step is to create a new one.

In our society we have decided that someone else who is more qualified, more holy, or more educated about spirituality in some way knows God better than we do. That's ludicrous and simply untrue. Absolutely every person is individually wired to know God in a way nobody else ever will. The more I understood this, the more it became vitally important for me to take the time to deeply know *my* God—the God of *my* being.

Trust me, you know the God of your being. You really do. In fact, nobody can be more of an expert in your God than you. But the key is getting you back to this amazing, perfect connection you have always had.

Getting a new God is not going to be easy—especially in the beginning. The resistance of the ancient mind, the ancestry that is encoded in your being and your own conditioning, is going to fight back. Know that these old voices are going to scream and argue, "Who are you to make up who God is?" "What if you're wrong and God really will throw you into hell?" "Why don't you play it safe and just go to church on holidays, show up when you have to, and just squeak by?" Fear will rise up quickly, but pay it no mind. It's time for it to dissolve into the nothingness from which it came.

Today, because I have taken the time needed to actively transform my beliefs and ideas about God, I now live in a completely new and expanded reality. I feel so free, loved, supported, protected, and at one with my creator. I have a loving, personal relationship that is alive, interactive, co-creative, and deeply fulfilling. I believe in myself more because I know at a deep level that God, the Infinite, the great I Am presence is within me, for me, all around me, forever. And yes, this new experience of God absolutely has freed me from suffering.

Let's look at some new ideas about God. Some may feel really good immediately. Others may make you pause and feel resistance. I encourage you to welcome those feelings. Breathe them in, but don't allow them to stop you. Just acknowledge them and be willing to have your mind and heart renewed.

Although we are one with God, and God is all we are, at our current state of consciousness and evolution the best way to get to know the God of your being is by establishing a conscious relationship. Your bond with God, like all relationships in your life, develops according to the time and commitment you put into it.

Your relationship with God is the most intimate one you can have, and the more you allow this intimacy to deepen, the more your other relationships will be expanded and blessed: easier, more fun, and more fulfilling. The more you depend upon God as your inner happiness, support, acknowledgment, source, and supply, the more you can allow other people in your life to be who they are with no expectations or need for them to be different.

Exercise: Hire Your New God

I'm going to take us back to the exercise about firing the old God. If you haven't completed that yet, please take the time to do that now, because it leads perfectly into this next part—creating a new, more expansive, only-for-you God. We do this by writing a God-for-hire advertisement. (If you need help then ask for it, right?) And how do you specifically get what you want, in God, and in life? By being specific and clear, of course.

This exercise, which I have done with countless people, is meant to be fun and transformational. This is where you get to create a God that is perfect for you. Remember, this God knows your every wish, desire, and need. This God loves what you love and wants you to experience and have what you love. This God, *your* God, is here for you. So if you love to shop, ask for a God that loves to shop. Create a God that loves to make love, eat chocolate, drive fast cars, surf, help others, paint, sing, dance. Create a God you can count on!

I want you to experience God as much as possible throughout your days, and the way to do that is to realize that when you are doing what you love, and your life is filled with joy and purpose, then you are one with God. There is a simple and very deep equation that sums this up:

When you feel good, you are feeling God.

Why? Because your God *is* your good. They are one and the same. I mean feeling authentically, naturally, and wholly good. I mean feeling goodness that makes the world a better place. Your God never can or will cause harm to another. Feeling your good must multiply the possibility for others to feel theirs. Otherwise, it's not the real deal.

Now it's time to write your God-for-hire ad. Here's an example for you.

God for Hire

This job is available to be filled immediately. This God must be 100 percent accepting of me and all my foibles, and must love me not only in spite of them, but including them. This God must leave no part of me unloved or unappreciated. This God must be available every day—morning, noon, and night.

This God must be bigger, bolder, and louder than any fear. This God must give me clear direction and turn up the volume so I am certain not to miss it. And when I choose to not listen, this God must immediately expand His/Her/Its love and make His/Her/Its message of care and guidance even clearer.

This God must love and accept absolutely everyone. Nobody can be left out of the eternal plan of freedom and happiness. This God must lead me to forgiveness quickly and easily. This God must especially help me know I am loved when I am feeling needy, insecure, and afraid.

The God of my being must have a great sense of humor, show magnificence in all things, help me be honest with myself and others, and never *ever* allow me to feel bad about my body, my weight, my age, or anything about me. Help me to take things lightly. Help me to always share. Protect me from the storms, and if I need to go through them, by all means, help me get my raincoat on and my umbrella up long before it's too late.

Apply in person, in my sleep, in the wind, or anywhere you want to. Just make sure I see it and feel it. This is a lifetime job with amazing benefits . . . me!

Now you write yours. Let it flow, and make it fun and meaningful. Feel free to copy parts of mine, but mostly make it your own and make sure you feel good after you've completed it. Read it out loud to yourself and say a huge YES to this. Read it often to help get you deeply related to this new, expanded declaration that says you are ready to be loved, supported, and connected to *your* God.

Building a Relationship with Your God

There are as many different ways to know God as there are people. Your way is all you need to discover. The great Indian guru Ramana Maharshi said, "Each one thinks of God according to his own degree of advancement. Worship God with or without form until you know who you are."

Some people actually like imagining God as a dear friend. Others really feel wonderful having a loving, nurturing, protective, and supportive mother or father image. Still others feel quite comfortable knowing God as a presence of light within and all around. The image doesn't matter. What does matter is that you be able to deeply and freely relate to your God—to talk, share, and, most importantly, really listen and hear the God of your being. Your personal God is a voice of inspiration, inner guidance, support, and divine direction. Some call it your intuition. Some call it your higher self. What matters is that what you call it feels right and good in your heart. As the saying goes, "A rose by any other name would smell as sweet."

You're actually quite used to listening to thoughts and voices in your head all day long. Most of them are not the voice of God. How can you tell the difference? It's simple—the voice is either loving or it's not. And if it's not loving, then it isn't your God.

As you are learning to listen for the voice of your God, you must pay attention to how it sounds and how it makes you feel. Your God will *never* judge, punish, unkindly push, or name anything about you wrong. Quite the opposite! The God of your being is the voice that celebrates you, adores you, and gives you clear guidance and direction. You just need to take the time to hear and discern it. When I realize an inner voice is starting to take on a tone that feels mean or impatient, I stop, breathe deeply, and say, "This is clearly not the voice of God, so I'm no longer listening."

Exercise: Pray to Your New God

Prayer is one of my favorite tools for deepening my relationship with God, as well as increasing my ability to manifest all my dreams and desires. With prayer, you can turbocharge your connection and communication with God.

There are many ways to pray, but what really matters is that you (1) ask from your heart; and (2) remain open, humble, and willing to receive. Prayer's deepest purpose is to change you. Prayer goes to work to make you a vibrational, energetic match for that which you desire. That's when your intent can become fulfilled. There are lots of formal ways to pray, and many of them are very good. I say just ask. Just talk to the God of your being with no pretense. Say, "Hey, this is really what I want. Please help me become that which I need to be so that I can have it." Every single morning I open my eyes and the first thing I say is, "Good morning, my Divine. Thanks for this day. I invite you to take the lead. Make this day be excellent, and most importantly, help me to see, hear, and know you in everything that occurs." Then throughout the day I take the time to think about God and say hello. Or, if I am in need of some advice or assistance in letting go of control, I just ask for it. I talk, talk, talk to my Divine. Mostly this happens in my head, but if I'm alone I sometimes speak out loud.

It is said that God hears and answers our prayers even before they are spoken. Think about that. Now, that is an extremely loving, generous, there-for-you-all-the-time kind of a God! I invite you to not question this, but instead say yes and see what it feels like to live from it. Say, "My prayers are always answered. My God loves me so much that even before I express my prayers they are done. I am so blessed! I am so blessed! I am so blessed!"

Finally, please never censor yourself when you are talking/praying to God. This is important. Get over the idea that God has to be spoken to in a certain way. If you're angry, share your anger. If you tend to swear, then by all means, speak the way you normally would. Don't try to be anything other than who you are. Your God doesn't give a squat about how you say what you say. Remember, your

God offers *unconditional* love and acceptance! This will create and maintain an authentic relationship, which is what you want.

Exercise: Journal with Your New God

One of my favorite ways to connect with my God is through journaling. I have a journal and two different colored pens sitting by my bedside and in my briefcase. I use one color to say hello to God and begin the conversation. I ask questions, share frustrations and inspirations—whatever is happening, I get it down on paper. Sometimes slowly and other times very quickly I will literally hear a voice within begin to speak. At that moment I switch to the other colored pen and allow that voice to say anything it wants to say. I breathe and just allow words of love and wisdom to flow through me and onto the paper. It is a magnificent experience.

For some, this practice produces results very quickly, meaning that the person finds him- or herself very capable of listening and actually hearing a voice of wisdom and love. For others, it takes some time, and it can feel like you might be faking it at first. I say allow yourself to fake it if that's what it feels like. So what. Allow yourself to be a beginner and let it come out sloppy. Let yourself be uncertain. I guarantee you that if you will just keep going to the page and creating the dialogue, you will begin to hear and sense that deeper wisdom rising up from within. You will notice that really great answers come to you. You will receive guidance to wait and be patient, or to take an action now. Your God will tell you to hug yourself, drink water, and take a nap.

Remember, what is mandatory at every turn is that this conversation with your God be loving. If there's any judgment or recrimination coming through, stop, close your eyes, and ask that only love speak. If you're still feeling stuck then take a break. Put the pen down, take a walk, and do something really, really nice for yourself.

Building your relationship with God takes time, commitment, and consistency. When you show up I am certain God will more than meet you halfway. It is said, "God is spirit, and those who worship him must worship in spirit." God is an ever-present source of life with no death, love with no fear, good with no bad. God is wholly inclusive of all that is. God is the universal spiritual laws that cause order, creation, and expansion. God is one indivisible, brilliant light in which absolutely everyone belongs, has purpose, and also has for the taking all that they desire— and even more than that.

When you begin to know God as this ever-pervading spirit, you open up to seeing God all around you: in nature, animals, other people, colors, flowers, and trees— in all and as all. When you know God as your never-failing source and substance, you are able to open up to multiple streams of wealth and opportunity because you know God is infinite and everywhere.

If you stay on your path of communing with, seeking, singing about, talking to, journaling to, and relating with the God of your being, there will come a moment when you say, from the innermost part of yourself, "Oh, *my* God." And you will feel this oneness, this spectacular light. Then, and trust me on this one, your suffering days are numbered.

With a new God in your heart, it's time to take a really, really powerful step in living a joyous, suffering-free life. It's called . . . forgiveness (insert big cheers of excitement here!). I love it! Forgiveness has changed my life in some of the most profound ways. How about letting it change yours, too?

2

Forgive Yourself and Others

When you hold resentment toward another,
you are bound to that person or condition by
an emotional link that is stronger than steel.
Forgiveness is the only way to dissolve that
link and get free.

—Catherine Ponder

In 1981, the mother of Michael Donald, a nineteen-year-old African American who was tortured and killed by two members of the KKK, sat in a courtroom listening to testimony from one of her son's murderers. James Knowles, the young man on the stand, turned to Mrs. Donald with tears in his eyes and said, "I hope you can forgive me for what I have done to your son." She rocked back in her chair, looked him in the eyes, and replied, "Son, I've already forgiven you."

This woman had suffered the greatest loss of her life, and yet she allowed love and mercy to set Knowles free from the personal torment of his horrific mistake. It may have taken Mrs. Donald a very long time to grieve the loss of her son, but in her soul she became free the moment she spoke those words. Morris Dees, her lawyer, said, "The words that came out of her mouth were a higher justice than the seven million dollars she was rewarded for her loss."

How does someone find the strength to allow the grace of forgiveness to flow through so generously in such trying times? Can you even imagine how you would respond if you were in her shoes? I know there have been plenty of times in my life when finding the willingness to let go and forgive was deeply challenging, even though what I was called to forgive was nothing close to the tragedy Mrs. Donald endured.

What Is Forgiveness?

Forgiveness is a *spiritual practice* that frees you from the prison of regret and brings victory over every victim experience. It clears away the anguish that blame brings and ultimately ends the blame game altogether. It removes the filters of judgment that block you from being able to see the present moment goodness and possibilities within yourself, others, and the world. It heals a broken heart and restores it to unconditional love and acceptance. It is the practice that allows you to look into the eyes of the person who caused you great pain and say, with all the love in your heart, "I forgive you" . . . and mean it.

The practice of forgiveness causes a quantum leap in consciousness that frees you from guilt and the false belief in duality (God vs. the devil, good vs. bad, right vs. wrong). It returns the mind of the forgiver to its natural state of oneness, which is the spiritual reality behind all that is happening. Ultimately forgiveness is for the *giver*, and it is a key step to ending suffering in your life.

How Do You Forgive?

I spent my twenties stuck in a lot of emotional pain and suffering. My childhood was rough, and I had a lot of pent up resentment and anger. When faced with this kind of situation, some people act out their pain, while others turn it upon themselves. I did the latter.

I remember the day my minister said to me, "You've got to forgive. It's your only way out."

"How the heck do you do that?" I asked.

I really had no clue.

My minister was so kind and compassionate with me during that time when I really could not get my life to work. In answer to my question of how to forgive, he told me that the help would come the very moment I was willing to simply ask. He said, "Even an ounce of willingness is enough." It would have to be. It was all I had.

Later that evening, I was sitting in my bed and I said out loud to God, "Look, I don't know how to do this, and most of me doesn't want to. But I feel like crap and am getting nowhere fast on my own. So you're going to have to meet me where I am. I can only do what I can do, and right now it doesn't feel like much . . . but I'm here."

I asked. My words were far from perfect, but I did it. Fortunately for you and me, the power of love that does the forgiving is generous and always happy to respond. I didn't necessarily feel the gates of heaven open, but I did feel something stir that if it had a voice would have said, "I'm here. I've got this!" That night my life started turning and changing in the right direction.

So many of us believe that the onus of forgiving falls squarely and completely on us, and us alone: *I'm the one who has to suck it up and set the one who hurt me free. I have to be the bigger person and just act as if (fill in the blank) never happened.* This kind of thinking is the exact opposite of how it works. The freedom comes in the revelation that you alone *cannot* forgive. The human part of you that was hurt or victimized is not capable of forgiving, nor should it be expected to be. That would be like falling into a thirty-foot hole and expecting yourself to get out on your own. You can't. You need someone to throw you a rope. When it comes to forgiveness, that rope is the Holy Spirit,

God, your higher power, the Divine, or whatever name you choose.

There is one more step after you ask, which is to let go and surrender the how, when, and where it happens. Your part, to the best of your ability, is to refrain from thinking about the situation as well as from getting emotionally hooked into the story. For me, I keep it real simple. When the thought of the specific incident or person comes to mind and begins to seduce me into the anger, self-righteousness, and suffering, as quickly as possible I say, "Holy Spirit—take this now! Remove this from my mind and set me free!" Sometimes I need to repeat that several times until I feel some relief. This is a process, not a one-time event.

How Often Should We Forgive?

It is written in the Bible that Jesus was asked how often we are to forgive. His response was 70 x 7. As a child, that was perfectly clear to me: Someone had 490 chances. That seemed exceedingly generous, and way more than I'd ever seen anyone forgive. Now, who knows what happens at 491. I guess that's when you could officially never forgive again, right? Wrong!

Seven is a mystical number. It is said the world was created in seven days. The Israelites walked for seven days and seven nights around the walls of Jericho, and the walls came tumbling down. There are seven days in the week, seven chakras, and seven colors in the rainbow. The number seven appears throughout ancient and current culture as a number that represents completion.

To forgive 70 x 7 times is a transcendent answer to a human question. To be directed to forgive 70 x 7 represents infinite forgiveness—forgiving until forgiveness is no more. This is so much greater than anything our human mind can comprehend, and yet our spirit within, the wholeness of God that has never been harmed, understands and easily agrees.

This approach does not speak so much to a single incident but to a practice that ultimately will cleanse our consciousness of all beliefs in separation, guilt, and victimization. Forgiveness is a tool we have been given by the Holy Spirit to awaken us to our wholeness, our holiness. In this holiness all suffering ceases.

Exercise: The 70 x 7 Forgiveness Circle

I created the following exercise to facilitate a shift in consciousness as you build a solid foundation for a life free of suffering. This exercise is to be done over seven days, but if it takes longer, that's OK. This is not about hurrying on to the next step. Remember, everything you do from here on will rest on this rock of forgiveness, so make it solid, enormous, and indestructible.

To start, imagine seven concentric circles, each representing a different layer of the relationships in which you live:

> Your God

> Yourself

> Your family

> Your intimate relationships—spouses, lovers, or friends

> Your acquaintances, associates, and other distant connections

> The establishment—companies and institutions

> Your beliefs—individual and collective

We'll cover each circle one by one, starting with the most personal inner circle, God, and eventually ending up with the outermost circle, the world at large—other people, organizations, beliefs, and collective agreements. Each day, you will write a prayer of forgiveness, beginning with the innermost circle and working your way outward. You'll read the same prayer ten times throughout the day for one week. Multiply those seven circles times ten repetitions, over the course of seven days each, and you have your 70 x 7.

Feel free to use my templates below if they help you in getting started with your own prayers, but give yourself permission to write whatever feels right. Your words and your willingness are the most powerful tools you have. Allow yourself to uncover your true feelings. Tap into your heart. Cry, yell, swear, release! Let go, and let God do for you and through you that which you have been praying for—freedom.

One final tip: Be sure to include throughout each prayer the recognition that it is God, the Divine Presence, Love, or whatever name you use, that does the work. You are the willing vessel and the recipient of its fulfillment.

Let's begin with the first circle.

Circle 1: Your God

We did a lot of great work on getting a new God in the last chapter, but it always helps to lock it in with a powerful letter of forgiveness. Here's an example, but again, please use your own words to reflect your feelings and intentions. Trust your inner self to guide you—you'll be amazed at how deep and clear your letters will be.

I, (name), ask that forgiveness be done through and for me in relationship to God. I ask that all false, fear-based beliefs be completely uprooted and dissolved. I ask that forgiveness wash away every negative idea about God and our relationship.

I ask that every day I know the God of my being more and more and trust this presence to work through me and for me in every area of my life. I ask that forgiveness set me free to be loved, adored, nurtured, and nourished by God. I want to create a new, intentional, and fun relationship with God so that forgiveness clears the way.

By the power of this prayer and intention, I ask that forgiveness release me from all my dualistic beliefs about God and that I may know God in and as oneness. May I be deeply healed from any lies or limitations that I have placed upon God.

I am renewed by the power of this prayer. I am free to love God, to know God, to trust God, and to allow God. Truly, I let go and I let God. And so it is. And so it shall be.

Circle 2: Yourself

I, (name), ask that total forgiveness be activated within me and for me. I ask that I be freed from every judgment and limitation I hold against myself. For every lie I have ever told, I ask that forgiveness free me from the ripples of their effect and that I be lifted into my full integrity, always confident to speak my truth with love and clarity.

I ask that forgiveness flow through me specifically for my body temple. I open to allow all the abuses, words, and actions that my body has endured to be healed.

For everything I have ever done, said, or thought that is less than holy, less than grateful, and out of alignment with my integrity, for all the ways I have hurt others and myself, known and unknown, I ask that forgiveness heal them and me so that only care and connection remain.

Holy Spirit, please set into motion the power of forgiveness, for in my ignorance and fear I know not what I do. Please let the power of forgiveness set me completely and forever free from the past. It is over! And so it is. And so it shall be.

If you are burdened with the suffering of self-hatred and inner-directed judgment, please focus on just this circle for a whole week. Take the time to read this prayer only ten times a day for seven days, each time slowly and with intention. Create a sacred space for yourself by lighting a candle and closing out the rest of the world. After a week has passed, you can pick up with the other circles of the exercise for the full 70 x 7 cycle.

Circle 3: Your Family

I, (name), by the power of this intention and prayer, ask that forgiveness occur for my family, immediate and extended, for anything they have done to me that has been less than loving, kind, and for my highest good.

I realize that my parents and family members have often acted out of their own beliefs, fears, and insecurities. Underneath these there is only love. I realize that we are one in this love, and it is no mistake that we are family.

From this day forward I choose to unconditionally love my family and appreciate them for who they are. I forgive them, and I ask to be renewed so I see them as God sees them—innocent and free.

By the power of my own word and my oneness with God, they are forgiven. I am forgiven. We are forgiven. Here and now I am made anew. And so it is. And so it shall be.

Circle 4: Your Intimate Relationships—Spouses, Lovers, or Friends

I, (name), ask that forgiveness be activated within me for my spouse, lover, or friends for the following:

(Name), for the lies he/she has told me. For the misuse and abuse of my (list here—let it all out), and for all the times that in our fear we have been unkind to each other. Help me to see and love this person as you do.

Please bless and forgive every person close to me who has used me intimately to escape their own pain. Shower them with love, peace, and joy. Please bless and forgive me for using others to escape my own pain.

I ask God to forgive my closest friends, (name them). For anything that has occurred between us that is less than loving, please, God, forgive them and help me to see them as you do—innocent and free.

Dear God, dear Universe, please let the power of forgiveness set my loved ones and me completely and forever free from the past. And so it is. And so it shall be.

Circle 5: Your Acquaintances, Associates, and Other Distant Connections

I, (name), ask that forgiveness be activated for myself and those who have treated me less than kindly, ma de fun of me, thought less of me, and degraded me in any way. I ask that forgiveness set free anyone who failed to see my brilliant light and the greatness within me, especially (name teachers, bosses, coworkers, etc.).

Anyone who has spoken about me negatively, known or unknown, I ask that forgiveness set them and me free. Truly, in fear they know not what they do.

I ask the loving power of God to forgive everything that has occurred, cleansing me on every level of my being. By the power of my own word and my oneness with God, they are forgiven. I am forgiven. We are forgiven. And so it is. And so it shall be.

Circle 6: The Establishment—Companies and Institutions

By the power of this prayer and intention, I, (name), ask God to activate the healing power of forgiveness for all establishments, organizations, and institutions that I have judged and put outside my heart. Being manmade, they have limited me or projected upon me ideas about who and what I am supposed to be. I forgive them for judging me as being inadequate and flawed in any way.

I forgive the religions that taught me there is a separation between God and me. I forgive them for abusing their power and wielding it over innocent people. I forgive them for hurting people and making them feel unworthy.

I forgive the school systems of my youth and all those who are trapped in it, perpetuating a system that doesn't honor the entirety of the students. I forgive my government, and I forgive myself for seeing them as arrogant, selfish, narrow-minded, and fear-based. I forgive all political and national leaders around the world and all entities that act out of hatred and fear.

I forgive any and all corporations that are operating out of greed at the expense of our environment and people's lives. I forgive the arrogance of the medical system and know that doctors and nurses are only human, trapped by false beliefs like everyone else.

I affirm the truth that God is with all of us! Dear loving Universe—please let the power of forgiveness set us completely and forever free from the past and the stories of separation. Oneness prevails. And so it is. And so it shall be.

Circle 7: Your Beliefs—Individual and Collective

I, (name), ask that forgiveness be done through me for all beliefs of separation that exist with me and the collective field of humanity.

By the power of this prayer and intention, I ask that forgiveness release me from all my dualistic beliefs about men, women, blacks, whites, Jews, Muslims, Christians, atheists, the educated and the undereducated, the rich and the poor, the young and the old, the attractive and the ugly, the skinny and the fat, and every other judgment or idea of people that is less than loving, supportive, and holy.

I sincerely ask that I be given new eyes to see a world where we truly are One. Where there is hate, sadness, and loneliness, please help me to be the consciousness of love and inclusion so that every person feels connected and better about him- or herself.

I ask that all compulsive and addictive thoughts and ways of being be forgiven and released from my consciousness.

Specifically I ask to be relieved from (list specific addictions related to you or your family, or addictions that you have a prejudice about).

I ask that fear be forgiven and that I be freed from all the ways that it traps me, others, organizations, groups, nations, religions, and the world. I ask that I may recognize it and transform it with love.

I allow forgiveness to set me free, to lift me into a consciousness of oneness. Dear God, dear Loving Universe . . . please let the power of forgiveness set me and everyone else completely and forever free. And so it is.

Congratulations. If you have completed the seven days of forgiveness, I am pretty certain you are feeling lighter, more open, and more present to your life and its many blessings.

It's important to remember what I mentioned earlier—forgiveness is not a one-time deal. Forgiveness is a process and a practice. It is an art as much as a tool, and like all artistic expressions, the more you do it the better you become. Be willing to do it incorrectly, fall down, and get right back up again.

When you are feeling angry, afraid, guilty, ashamed, or separate, be quick to call upon forgiveness. Forgive yourself for believing you are separate, and ask, ask, ask the Holy Spirit to reveal its perfect love right where you are . . . right now. It works!

In this chapter we've laid a powerful foundation for your freedom from suffering. Getting a new God and allowing forgiveness to cleanse your mind, body, and spirit is necessary for you to take the next step in your journey toward joy.

3

Love Yourself
Madly

It's not your job to like me . . . it's mine!

—Byron Katie

*To love yourself right now, just as you are, is
to give yourself heaven.*

—Alan Cohen

In an interview on *The Oprah Winfrey Show,* Jane Fonda
revealed that it wasn't until after she turned sixty that
she realized one of life's most important secrets: She
had to give up her incessant desire to be perfect so that
she could begin to experience herself as whole.

Jane Fonda has proven herself to be so much more
than just a talented actress—she cares about people and
has used her wealth and recognition to do much good

in the world. She is stunning, successful, smart, and powerful; but despite all her success, here she is telling America's most popular talk show host that she has always viewed herself as unattractive and not good enough. For years she suffered from an ever-present belief that so many of us share: the "I am not enough" fallacy.

As I listened to her, I realized how pervasive the obsession with being perfect is in our culture. Perfection is unattainable, and though we may say we know this, it doesn't stop us from rejecting and abusing ourselves when we fail to achieve it. I can relate to Jane Fonda's insatiable need to succeed and become somebody special. I thought that once everyone loved and respected me then I could finally, hopefully feel OK. I never stopped long enough to realize I was never going to feel good, because I was trapped in a barrage of negative messages I was telling myself. Daily I berated myself for not being good-looking or thin enough, smart or young enough, organized or productive enough. Sometimes I articulated these beliefs out loud, but mostly they were like a low-grade, constant hum in my subconscious mind.

The BIG Lie: Be Like Everyone Else and Then You'll Be Loved

Growing up, I really didn't love or accept myself. I was never taught how. My parents didn't know how to truly love and honor themselves; neither did my grandparents, or their parents, or probably their parents. I came from generations of people who did not know what deep, fulfilling love and acceptance of self meant, let alone how to do it. And as I watched Jane Fonda talk about her journey of awakening to what she called her wholeness, I realized that most of the world is missing this necessary piece.

Why does it take sixty years for someone to discover that self-love and acceptance is where real fulfillment lies? That their needs are important, and, even more, that nobody is ever going to fulfill them unless they first deem themselves worthy—not just in word, but in deep knowing?

Since before you can remember, you have been learning the rules of the world—what makes people accept or reject you. Being that you were brilliant and wanted and needed to be loved, you started discerning from an early age who you could and couldn't be in relationship to the world around you. Not who you *are*, but who you were *supposed to be*. We have been taught to act in a way that is beneficial for Mom, Dad, family, friends, and society—but the conclusions we make and the actions we take based on outside influences sometimes don't match. And we've all experienced many moments where there was a big difference between the two.

You were told how to behave, what to say, and how to fit into society's rules. You were rewarded for being "good" and polite; and you were admonished for saying you thought Aunt Sally was fat and mean. Before you could even begin to comprehend the game called Fit In At All-Costs, you were playing it. You decided, according to how the adults around you responded, which parts of you were lovable and which ones were not. You started slicing and dicing yourself in order to please, be accepted, and belong. Don't worry, you weren't alone—everyone was doing it!

As you grew older, the messages about what you needed to do began to take on a different flavor, one geared toward making a living. When you were five, it was OK to want to be a ballerina, or a professional baseball player. It made the adults smile and give you a loving pinch on the cheek. But as you grew into your teens, it stopped being so cute. Eventually you were probably asked to find a "more reliable" way of supporting yourself in the future.

Perhaps college comes and goes, and soon it's time to get married, which means it's time to choose one person to love and be attracted to for the rest of your life. Perhaps over the years your marriage becomes less and less fulfilling—but this too must be kept a secret. "Marriage is a compromise," you're told. So you keep on keeping on and doing what you have been taught, all the while pressing your personal wants and fantasies down deeper and deeper.

Next thing you know, kids come along, and now it's time to teach them the rules of the world so they too can fit in, not rock the boat, be polite, be acceptable, and succeed. Suddenly you're sixty years old and saying to yourself, "Who am I? What is important and true for me? . . . I have no idea!"

Even if your life is very different from this story—perhaps you never married, or are happily married; maybe you never had kids, or are gay or single, or are career-focused—it matters not. The common theme is that we all were trained in one way or another to abandon ourselves in bits and pieces along our journey.

The problem is that our society is outmoded; self-respect is considered selfish, and self-admiration is arrogant. We confuse self-care with vanity and consider self-appreciation unnecessary and indulgent. We are expected to downplay our accomplishments and be self-deprecating when a compliment comes our way. We are expected to not need, want, or dream . . . basically, we are expected to not be ourselves.

We have a deep fear that if other people really knew what we were thinking, if we told our truth, and if we chose to put ourselves first above others, they would not like us and perhaps ridicule and even abandon us. In many families and cultures around the world, people are literally shunned—banned from their own families, villages, and communities—because of their personal truth and choices. So for many this fear is deep and real.

The BIGGER Truth:
Be Yourself and You Are Love

We are in the new era, and the time to love and accept yourself first and foremost is now. We don't need to be in a retirement home before we awaken to the truth that once we finally give ourselves the acceptance and affirmation we've been wanting from the world and not getting, we suddenly feel . . . *whole.* Imagine what the world would be like if everyone truly loved themselves and sourced their own affirmation, recognition, and respect from within. Why, it would be heaven on earth.

Do you want to wait until your golden years to finally say, "I'm lovable and deeply deserving of my own respect and admiration"? I certainly don't, and the people over sixty whom I have talked to about this do not advise waiting, either.

This may be a new idea, but what's true is that every time you look *outside* yourself for love, recognition, or approval, you are abandoning yourself. The world says love comes from another, but the truth is you cannot give or receive love at all until you have it first for yourself. *A Course in Miracles* calls the predominant kind of love we experience in the world "special love." It's special because it needs someone distinct to give it to. It's special because it says, "You are mine and that other person is not." Special love separates and divides. It causes pain and loneliness. It is neediness, fear, and possession masquerading as real love.

In contrast, real love connects, shares, and expands. *A Course in Miracles* calls this "holy love" because it reveals the wholeness inside and needs no special person to bring it to life. Holy love is in you and me. It is always available and is not contingent upon any person, place, or thing. Once awakened, holy love can be shared with others without possessing them. Holy love casts an enormous net that includes absolutely everyone and excludes no one.

When it comes to loving ourselves, most people only practice special love. Within ourselves we make special the things about our personality, physical body, and emotional self that the world affirms while we disown the parts that are deemed unacceptable. Our healing comes in casting a net of holy love over our entire self that allows every single, separated part to come home into the light of acceptance. Suffering ends when you purposefully, powerfully, and passionately love all of yourself.

Tolerance will not do. Deeming yourself "OK" is not even close. I'm talking about a level of self-care that you most likely have not seen or been taught how to do. I'm talking about a whole new paradigm of self-love, appreciation, admiration, and adoration. I'm talking about pouring it on so thick that you just can't get enough of yourself! I'm talking about deep transformation that makes you go, "Oh my God! I wouldn't want to be anybody else in the entire world."

Break Out of Your Psychological Suffering

Carl Jung, the world-renowned psychiatrist and psychotherapist, said, "The most terrifying thing is to accept oneself completely." It's scary because total self-acceptance includes the inner terrains of our being—specifically our minds, where enormous amounts of self-recrimination and judgment reside and recycle. To change this mode of internal suffering requires us to begin listening to what we are thinking and saying to ourselves in a nonreactive way. What we discover as we begin exploring this inner landscape is that the voices are angry, mean, and indeed terrifying. They are anything *but* loving.

These voices of self-rejection, self-punishment, blame, guilt, and unworthiness are like ugly creatures living on the bottom of a swamp. They stay low until the water is stirred, at which time they immediately awaken and surface only to sabotage and cause trouble . . . *Who do you think you are? You're going to look like an ass, trust me. You're a phony—a fake. You're stupid/fat/mean/a bitch/a bully. You will not succeed!*

Because you've spent your life avoiding these voices and not confronting them, they have become real to you.

What makes it even harder is that they are powerful at convincing you that they are true. Listening to their chorus of judgments makes you want to run—but this time you can't. To become happy and at home within yourself is truly worth the effort, no matter how scary it may feel in the beginning.

Every unkind and unloving voice in your head is nothing more than a ghost from the past. You can't change the past, but you can realize that it has no real power of its own. *You* give the voices of suffering power by believing them, and therefore you have the power to become free from them. Consider this question: Who would you be if you were no longer running from, and crippled by, those negative voices? What would be possible for you if you were your very own best friend, lover, confidant, supporter, and number-one champion?

The reality is that you are not stupid, unlucky, mean, selfish, afraid, jealous, possessive, shy, uncaring, unattractive, unlovable, or un-anything! Sure, you have thoughts and feelings that say you are. But remember, you are a divine creation of that one magnificent life called God. Any and every silly quirk that makes you think or feel or act other than this truth is temporary—its days are over as soon as you choose to start believing something more kind and magnificent about yourself.

Your conscious mind is a magnificent tool that can be used for good! It is a miracle-making machine from which you can create absolutely anything you want—if you believe. So why not believe you are actually who you *really* are underneath all that made up, limiting, smelly garbage you've been thinking, saying, and imagining? Why not believe you are a divine expression of the all-good, infinitely brilliant, forever-expanding God?

This is not arrogant—quite the opposite. To know yourself as this presence and power of perfect love is humbling, heart-opening, and soul-expanding. To know yourself as the brilliant light of love is to know who you *really* are.

The way to become free from these negative thoughts, and the psychological suffering they bring, is by shining the light of love upon them. Practice seeing them as scared little children who need love, not aggression. Hear these voices as cries for healing and acceptance. When you hear and feel them, that's the time to take a deep breath and say, "My Divine, please take this thought and transform it with your love. And please heal the effects of it on every level of my being, that I may awaken to the love that I truly am. Let love heal—right here."

The more you can observe and surrender, the faster these voices will dissolve. And for those that don't, you'll discover you have a muscle of love that can allow them to rise up and be seen but not acted upon. You can just say, "Hello. What do you need?" Then listen . . . the voice will tell you what it wants. Just asking and listening is amazing self-care. Perhaps you can do something for yourself in that very moment that will be loving and nurturing. Perhaps you'll need to tell this part of yourself to wait until later. If you do, then please be sure to follow through on that promise. Leaving yourself hanging or not coming through for yourself will only continue the suffering. Each loving act and commitment fulfilled will transform your psychological suffering like nothing else can.

Love, Love, Love Your Body

One of my students became very disciplined in journaling with her Divine, and one day she said to me, "I'm so surprised. Continually the guidance I am getting is to drink water, take a nap, go for a walk, eat my vegetables, and give myself a big hug! I feel like my Divine is my grandmother!"

I wasn't surprised by this news at all. Taking care of your body temple is usually the first direction that comes from your Divine. You are the vessel through which the goodness of life pours, and if you're not caring for yourself then it *can't* flow. The God of your being can only do *for* you what it can do *through* you. This is a very important idea. If you do not care for yourself, you become like a pipe that is clogged, and just as water can only flow through at the force that the pipe will allow, the goodness of the Universe can only flow according to how open and clear you are.

Health is wealth, and taking care of your body is the most primal, basic way to practice self-love. When you stop to really listen to your body and seek guidance from within, it usually becomes crystal clear what you should do or not do, eat or not eat. Your body knows what it wants and needs. The challenge is in listening to your body and honoring its requests. As you open to listening more closely to your body you may find yourself needing to withdraw certain sugars, wheat, meats, or toxins that it has become addicted to. Once those are gone, wow! The communication between you and your body will likely improve tremendously.

Taking care of your body takes extra time because what it needs is not microwaved, fast and easy, non-food in a box, but living foods that require time to shop for and prepare. But this time is well spent, as it is always an expression of self-love. You are worth the time it takes to have the right foods around you.

In addition to putting what you need *into* your body, also remember that your body loves to move and feel good. Like a brilliant race car, your body loves to be used for what it was designed for. The truth is that the more we use our bodies in ways that make us feel healthy and strong, the better we feel on all levels of our being.

The world of exercise options is enormous. I guarantee you there is something out there you will really enjoy. For example, just the other day I saw an ad for fly yoga, which is a combination of traditional yoga techniques, acrobatics, gymnastics, and dance. They use silk hammocks and practice advanced inversions and circus-style tricks. How crazy fun is that? Not for you? Then how about joining a gym with a pool? Or riding your bike around town? There are lots of options, and you can switch up your routine based on the seasons.

Whatever belief is keeping you from this kind of care, give it up. If you think you've got no time, you're wrong. You choose how to spend your time—so reallocate it. If you're waiting for your body to be in better shape *before* you'll start exercising, seriously and quickly give that one up! That's just a setup to keep you not exercising. If you're one of those people who says, "I hate exercise," then definitely give that statement up. Literally surrender it and decide for yourself that there is something fun and deeply fulfilling for you and your body. Everyone has to move.

When you make this proactive decision, I assure you that something will appear before you. Either a friend will casually mention something or you'll see it right in front of your face on a billboard. There is something—I absolutely know it. And remember, you are worth it!

While healthy eating and exercise may have the bonus effects of making you slimmer and healthier looking, it's important not to lose sight of why you're taking better care of yourself in the first place. Many want their body to be different—sexier, thinner, more muscular, whatever. But dieting and exercising for the sole purpose of superficial gain will not keep you motivated in the long run, because placing your worth on other people's recognition is not sustainable. And that illusion of having a supermodel or action hero's body only leads to one thing: *extreme suffering*. I think most of us, especially in the Western world, have these beliefs to a certain degree.

To those who are deeply suffering in this area, there is help. Begin with admitting your powerlessness and ask to become willing to get the help you need. It will appear when you are ready.

For many of us, this is not a life-or-death situation, but more of a chronic, low-grade form of suffering. It's time to address it head on and stop it, and the way to do that is by choosing to end any and all negative, unkind, and unproductive statements about your body. Who would you be if you were free of any and all negative attacks on your body temple? Just take a moment and breathe into this idea. What would be possible for you if you chose to love and accept yourself exactly as you are, right this very moment?

Your body needs and deserves your care and attention. It works so hard every day, and it never criticizes you—don't judge it, blame it, attack it, and stuff it with non-foods. Let's put down the boxing gloves and start loving it, touching it, appreciating and celebrating it.

Your body is an expression of what you think, say, do, and consume. It is an intelligent system that serves you while you are here on this earth. So, not just caring for your body but treating it as a beautiful, worthy temple will transform the way you love and accept yourself. But remember, you are not *only* your body. When you die you will lay it down and let it go. It's important to keep this relationship in perspective.

I know there will come a time when loving yourself comes easily. But until then, we've got some practicing to do. The exercises in this chapter are meant to be ongoing until they become a way of life. There really is no day but today, so dive in and start loving all over yourself.

Exercise: Love Letter to Yourself

As you can see, I'm a huge fan of journaling and writing letters. This particular letter is one of my favorites to write, because it's so deeply healing. The purpose of this letter is to give yourself all the love, acceptance, affirmation, and appreciation you can muster—and then throw even more on top of that! I spent many years waiting for Mom, Dad, siblings, partners, lovers, and friends to say the words that would heal me. They said them—but they *didn't* necessarily heal me, because first I had to believe them.

You, and you alone, must love yourself madly. The paradox is that when you do, the world will reflect this back to you, and you'll be able to really breathe it in and enjoy it. Here's a sample letter to myself.

> Dear Mark Anthony,
>
> I absolutely love and adore you. You are just fantastic. You're smart, funny, attractive, and such a blessing to so many. You have no idea how much your positive approach to life helps others. I so honor how you survived some very rough times and are now a loving, compassionate man who is free from bitterness and filled with beauty and God's grace. Your willingness to keep growing and looking at yourself is amazing—seriously, the entire Universe rejoices at how open you are to see, change, expand, and allow greater good to be yours. I love you. I love you. I love you to the moon and back, to Mars and back, to Pluto and back, and to every star in the sky . . . and back. Don't ever wonder if you're lovable, because dang . . . YOU ARE! Please, enjoy your life. Look around and see how magnificent it is. You are here, now, and it is so, so damn good. All the love that you seek is within. All the joy that you want to feel is right inside you awaiting your calling. Be happy—now. Be willing to be more and more supported. Be content in knowing that you are deeply and dearly and fully loved.
>
> Sincerely,
> Myself

Now it's your turn. See if you can go even further and get even sappier than I did. Pour the love on real thick! Oh, by the way, don't just write it and put it away. Like your forgiveness circles, you'll want to read this letter morning, noon, and night for twenty-one whole days. Then what? Write a new one . . . and start over.

Exercise: Mirror, Mirror on the Wall, Who's Amazing After All?

Stand in front of a full-length mirror naked. Begin by looking into your eyes and just breathe. Take some slow, deep breaths until you feel your body relax. Beginning with your eyes, say, "Thank you, eyes. I love and appreciate you."

Repeat this as you move to different parts of your body—your nose, mouth, cheeks, hair, ears, throat, shoulders. Move all the way down your body, slowly and intentionally. Tell every part of your body, "Thank you. I love and appreciate you." Include your vital organs, your skin, your bones, and your fluids. Do not stop until you have covered every body part from head to toe.

When you've covered everything, stand there a few minutes longer just breathing and looking at yourself. Refrain from judgment. Just be with yourself. Look at yourself. When was the last time you just looked at yourself and poured love upon your body temple? Please, be extremely, outrageously kind.

If I were to choose the most important exercise in this book it would be this one. It's vulnerable, yes, but also transformational.

Exercise: Pamper Yourself!
And Then Do It Some More!

Loving yourself means treating yourself like royalty as often as you can. Get a massage, take long walks, take yourself out on a date, or see a movie by yourself. Basically, be with you! The more time you spend caring for yourself, the more you'll like being alone with yourself. Even when life gets hectic and it seems you just can't get ahead, give yourself the time, attention, and care you deserve.

What makes you feel pampered and special? You don't need a lot of money to do this. Bubble baths with candles burning and music you love can be heaven on earth. Discover the healthy foods you love and have them around you as much as possible. Do the same with people and things.

Once a month, give yourself a full "Me Day" where you only do what you want to do when you want to do it—for and by yourself. Oh, the rewards that will come out of this are countless.

Remember, loving yourself is a daily practice that will keep getting easier and easier the more you do it. It's a powerful step in ending unnecessary suffering. It's also a step that triggers the perfectionist within that says, "See, you can't even do that right." Even that voice must be loved and accepted into your heart. Remember, there is nothing—absolutely nothing—about you that is unacceptable to your personal God.

As we continue, I invite you to imagine yourself as a little child—when you were free to dream, play, and make-believe. Remember what it was like to want what you wanted for the sheer joy of wanting it. This is the next place we must go to release a whole stash of suffering.

4

Want What
You Want

*Ask and it will be given to you; seek and you
will find; knock and the door will be opened
to you. For everyone who asks receives; the one
who seeks finds; and to the one who knocks,
the door will be opened.*

—Matthew 7:7–12

Ask and it will be given to you." This ancient quote
holds the key to ending so much of your suffering. It is a promise of support, abundance, and
great freedom. To the child in us, it feels like Santa Claus
is real. To the truth seeker, it offers guidance. And for
those who desire healing from pain and suffering, it gives
not only hope but a miracle.

I think of this Universe as a yes machine. It's the only
response it ever gives. Whatever we desire to accomplish,

have, or be, it simply and always says *yes*. The Universe cannot deny us anything, nor can it judge what we want. It cannot say, "Now, you know you don't really want that, so I'm not going to give it to you." It doesn't deem you selfish or foolish or greedy or stingy. It doesn't have the ability to discern right from wrong because it doesn't know right from wrong. It knows one thing . . . yes!

So why don't you have absolutely everything that your heart desires right now? Why do you find yourself wanting for certain things or experiences to no avail? Why do you find yourself at the end of the month struggling to pay the rent, fall in love, feel healthier, or do what really makes your heart sing?

The fact is that you were born naturally and joyously wanting. It was fun and easy for you. You saw beautiful things, cool things, tasty things. "I want it" was something you said multiple times a day. And the adults around you would smile and be proud of you for asking. Once in a while they would say no because you'd had enough or it wasn't good for you. You might have thrown a temper tantrum, but they picked you up and redirected your attention to something that would make you feel loved and happy again.

Then one day, although you're not sure exactly when it happened, your wanting became a nuisance. Suddenly "no" was delivered much more harshly, maybe even with a slap of the hand. That which was once so charming had new rules all around it, and you had to learn them real fast. Now, your wanting seemed to be making Mommy and Daddy unhappy, at times even angry.

I still remember shopping with my mom at a big store when I was five years old. Oh, the aisles were just filled with colorful things, toys, candy, and magic. I wanted everything! Why not? I was five, and everything was fantastic to me. I remember saying, "I want that . . . I want that . . . Mom, can I have that?" After a little while she turned and looked down at me. She was angry and frustrated, and she said, "We're going to leave this store right now if you don't stop! Why do you have to want everything you see? Stop being selfish."

I didn't know what "selfish" was, but I knew it wasn't good. From that day forward my natural joy of wanting became mixed up with a lot of uncertainty and fear. When was it OK to want? How much can I want without getting into trouble? When can I choose freely, and when do I choose what my parents, teachers, church, or peers think I should choose? What if what I really want makes people not like me or think I'm weird? What if my dreams are too big and I fail?

Can you see how over time our wanting becomes mixed with guilt, shame, fear, shoulds and shouldn'ts, judgments, and greed? That's a lot of gunk that gets laid on top of your ability to ask for what you want, seek and find, knock and open. Remember, the Universe says yes to all of it. That's why many of us have convoluted, dumbed down, mixed up stews of what we truly desire.

I'm Selfish—Yuck!

To be called "selfish" is painful. It cuts deep to feel the harsh judgment and disdain wrapped up in that word. It makes you feel wrong and shameful. It immediately makes you want to hide and erase whatever just happened that brought to you such an intense attack. When wanting something for yourself is judged so severely it can forever alter the way you view your needs and desires, causing you to hide and deny them.

In our society it is considered holy to be selfless and horrible to be selfish. Helping others is good, for sure, but not at the expense of your own well-being or the fulfillment of your heart's desires. Sure there are times when life calls us to help a sick friend or family member, or to sacrifice in the moment so another can move forward in their own life. But that is love in action, not suffering. To *sacrifice* means to "make sacred," and when we know it is right to postpone our own good for the moment we don't feel deprived—quite the opposite. We feel fulfilled. We feel the grace of God using us, and we are forever expanded by it.

To become free of suffering you must redefine the meaning of the word selfish. The truth is every one of us is selfish—every person on the planet has his or her own interest at heart, and that's the way it should be. You think of yourself and your needs all day long. You contemplate what you want, where to go, and who you want to be. It actually makes sense, since you're really the only person you can influence in these areas. It is your business to think about yourself, care for yourself, and want what you want, with no need to justify or explain it to anyone. My goal for you is that you become radically selfish and always check in with yourself first and foremost about what is good and true for you.

Your Mood Makes All the Difference

A percentage of your wanting comes from suffering—subtle and not-so-subtle beliefs of unworthiness, lack and limitation, doubt and worry. It makes sense—the discomfort is pushing you to want more, to change and grow. But not only does the Universe say yes to what you want, it also says yes to the core, generating ideas and feelings from which the wanting comes. For example, if you want to make more money, but you believe that you can't, don't know how, or aren't smart enough, then the Universe says, "Yes, you can't." "Yes, you don't know how." "Yes, you're not smart enough." Your basic desire for more money is good, but all the negative beliefs that swirl around it also get thrown into the fire of creation.

Because this is true, it's never a good time to want something when you are feeling fearful. Fear creates more fear. If you are trapped in thoughts of lack, feeling unlovable, regretting the past, anger, or worrying about the future then the first step is to become aware of your mind taking you down that fearful road. This is the time to take a breath and place your attention on what is happening in the present moment. Look for something good to focus on right where you are. The sun, a tree, a beautiful color—anything that can help shift your energy.

Fearful beliefs build their home in the cells of your body and create muscle memory, which is why your body automatically contracts when you feel afraid. For example, you will cross your arms, your leg muscles will tense up, your jaw will become clenched, your shoulders will lock, and your breathing can become shallow. You literally embody the fear. This is why getting up and moving your body is one of the best things you can do to shake you out of that fearful funk. Dance, sing, jump up and down, move your arms and legs into quirky positions—this will shift your energy like nothing else will.

Other times the best way out is through, which means the most self-loving choice will be to allow yourself to fully *have* your feelings, instead of changing them. Knowing whether to fully experience your feelings or change them requires you to tune in and listen to your personal Divine. Remember, your relationship with the God of your being is established, so if you don't know, ask, and you will be guided. If you sense that allowing yourself to be with your feelings is the right choice, then this is the time to release the wanting—at least for now. Say to yourself, "I am not going to focus on what I want right now. Instead I choose to be fully present to all that I am feeling." Invite your Divine to fill you with unconditional love, and then feel, feel . . . and feel some more. Don't deny yourself or judge the experience—just feel. It's very healing, indeed.

The key is to not have fearful feelings and want at the same time. If you're like most people, you've been doing this without even realizing it.

Everybody Has a Natural State of Wanting

Your wanting muscle may be over- or underdeveloped, depending on your upbringing. We learn how to want or not want from our parents and family. If those who raised you were happy and healthy in their wanting, able to manifest their desires while also not needing to have everything they want, then you were given a blueprint for successful wanting and its fulfillment.

If your parents put themselves into debt and suffering to fulfill their wanting, then you were given a blueprint that material things and "keeping up with the Joneses" will fulfill you. For some, this natural state of wanting is big and dramatic: desiring to travel the world first class, stay at the nicest hotels, and dine at the most elegant restaurants.

Or perhaps your family shunned any kind of dreaming or desiring for a better life with comments like, "Who do you think you are?" or "Why would you want that? What's wrong with what you have right now?" In this last case, you got a blueprint that keeps your wanting intensely under control and at a minimum.

Whether you were brought up to focus on your own comforts or helping others live a better life, there is no universal right or wrong way to want—there is only your right relationship to it. True freedom comes when you can fully embrace all that you want with no justifications, excuses, shame, or denial. Your body's hungers, fantasies, dreams, goals, visions, and hopes are all a wonderful part of who you are. Especially in the areas of money, sex, recognition, fame, and fortune, where embarrassment and judgments ride high, your freedom lies in allowing yourself to want what you want. No matter how crazy, outrageous, or even unacceptable it may seem, your desires must become totally acceptable to you. This is one of the greatest gifts you can give yourself.

I am not saying you are meant to *have* everything you want. It would be overwhelming and would actually cause *more* suffering if you got it all. There is an epidemic of people trying to fill a hole inside themselves with more and more things. In their need for safety, attention, instant gratification, or escape, their wanting becomes insatiable and out of control. Many people get themselves into horrific suffering because they think just because they want something they have to have it or even take it. Hoarding, spending more than you can afford, or causing pain and suffering to another because of your behavior is suffering, not freedom. In these cases, wanting is not the problem. This is the misunderstanding and misuse of wanting, coupled with deeper emotional problems, which lead to an addiction to the short-lived relief that possessing something brings.

Allowing yourself to want what you want, without causing any harm to yourself or another, will create within you a deep feeling of contentment that has nothing to do with having more. Inside this satisfaction you will love what you have. Enjoy your wanting, and at the same time be able to discern what is really important for you to acquire versus what is simply arising within, for the sheer joy of wanting.

Sally, a woman in her nineties, is probably the healthiest wanter I know. She is happy, active, and extremely interesting. She lives in a small one-bedroom apartment that is nicely furnished. She loves life and wants more of it. She knows she will never get all she wants, but she loves dreaming and imagining—it makes her feel so good. I naïvely asked her if she would ever be satisfied, to which she replied, "I am satisfied. Don't think because I want more that I'm not happy now. I love today and I can't wait for tomorrow." She lives in the perfect balance of loving what is while at the same time allowing herself to want and dream.

Exercise:
Let Your Full-Body Yes Be Your Guide

There are more options today than ever before, with even more coming our way. We now live in a world where the all-you-can-eat buffet is not only for food but also clothes, gadgets, travel, entertainment, you name it. "Do I really want this? Do I need it? . . . I don't know!" In all this overwhelm it can be hard to discern what you really want versus what is for your highest good.

I have a surefire way to help you get clarity. It's called having a full-body yes. We experience life on three levels: physical, mental, and emotional. When all three levels are in alignment with a resounding yes, you can be certain it is the right choice for you.

Let's say I am trying to decide if I want to go to dinner and a show with friends tonight. I close my eyes and take a few deep breaths. I say, "I am open and willing to hear what is deeply true for me." Then I place my hands on my head and ask, "Mental self, do I want to do this?" Then I listen for the answer. If it's a yes, it will be clear. If not, I take a moment and allow my mind to share why not.

If my mental self says yes, then I move to my emotional self by placing my hands between my stomach and ribcage (the seat of your emotional body) and ask, "Emotional self, do I want to do this?" and I listen. If I feel a no, then I listen for more information or guidance about why.

If I feel a yes, then I move on to the physical part of myself. I either stand up strong and tall or simply wrap my arms around myself and ask, "Body self, do I want to do this?"

Three yeses equals a full-body yes! At this point you can feel confident you are in alignment with what you want. This really does work for everything, from going to a movie to buying a new car, taking a new job, or having a critical conversation.

Inside you is what I call "the knower that knows," and its wisdom and guidance are available to you all the time and in every situation. It takes practice to hear and trust this inner knower, and faith to follow its guidance. But if you're willing, you can become a true expert at always knowing what you do and do not want in every situation.

When in doubt, simply ask, "Is this for my highest good and the good of all?" Does what you want expand your joy as well as bless those around you, or does it cause suffering somewhere, either now or at a later time? If you're willing to hear it, you will get the answer very quickly.

Time to Get Wanting!

Here is your new affirmation: "It brings my Divine great joy to fulfill my every dream and desire." I want you to memorize this and say it as often as you can. This affirmation is designed to reprogram your mind and energy to be receptive to the grace of God that is all around you. Remember, the God of your being loves you so much there are not enough words to express it. Whatever you desire, if it is for your greater good and the good of all, it is yours!

Exercise:
Work Through Your Unfulfilled Wants

Gather a few sheets of paper. On the first sheet, draw a vertical line down the center. On the left side, create a header called "What I Didn't Get That I Wanted" and on the right create a header called "Why." On the left list everything you can think of that you wanted but didn't get and on the right side write down why. This is not an intellectual exercise. This requires you to first pray to the God of your being and to invite Him/Her/It to guide you and speak through your heart. To truly know "why" something does or doesn't happen can be more complex than we can understand, but your intuition can give you a loving, clear answer that can be helpful. Here are some examples.

What I Didn't Get That I Wanted	Why
I did not get the ten-speed bike I wanted when I was twelve.	My parents genuinely could not afford to buy this for me, and I didn't know how to save money at that time in my life.
A puppy we had when I was young died shortly after we got him. I wanted so badly for him to live.	The puppy wasn't healthy, and it was best that he laid his body down. It was beautiful how my mother nursed him through the night and I stayed awake to help. The puppy felt very loved and cared for as he took his last breath.
I never became a dancer on Broadway.	I didn't have a strong enough focus and discipline to make this happen. It was a fantasy that I enjoyed thinking about, but my life did not genuinely align with this. In the most positive way, it wasn't meant to be.

Exercise: Appreciate Your Fulfilled Wants

In this exercise, you'll list all the things you *did* get and consider why you think you received them. Think of as many things as you possibly can. The goal of this exercise is to help you see how the Universe *is* answering your prayers and fulfilling many things you want.

What I *Did* Get That I Wanted	Why
I really wanted a keyboard for Christmas when I was about nine years old, and I got it.	My parents were happy to get me this gift because they knew I really wanted it and was excited to have it.
I applied for and was awarded a scholarship for college.	I worked very hard to get this. I had to audition, so I got extra help, practiced, and really showed up for it.
I found my perfect apartment the first time I lived alone as an adult.	I remember the moment I stepped into the apartment—I *felt* it was mine. The landlord told me it was already rented, but I knew. I told him to call me if anything changes. Three hours later he called telling me the person who was going to rent the place had backed out. It was so awesome! I loved that place.

After completing these exercises, take some time to reflect and write about what you discovered:

> Can you see the hand of God, or how the Universe was working for you in some of the things you did not receive?

> Did you discover any self-sabotaging patterns within yourself that perpetually keep you from getting what you want?

> Can you see how some things were just not meant to be, and that's OK?

> Is there anything on the list that could possibly still come to pass?

> Finally, is there anything unresolved?

If you have a close friend, prayer partner, counselor, or minister you deeply trust, I invite you to share both lists with that person and ask him or her to witness your life and revel in how this loving Universe is supporting you.

Exercise: Declare, Clarify, and Feel Good

This exercise is all about helping you get to why you want what you want. When you take the time to understand the feelings behind what you desire, you will begin to realize you are always seeking to feel good. You will also discover that you can create the feeling state you want, right now, without having exactly what you want. That will make you feel amazing, which in turn will accelerate your ability to get what you want!

This is a great exercise to do with a partner who is loving and supportive.

Sit directly across from your partner and set a timer for ten minutes. Have your partner ask you these three questions:

1. What do you really want?
2. What form do you see it taking? (Give me some details.)
3. How do you feel?

Answer your partner, and once you've cycled through the questions repeat through them again and again until time is up. All your partner needs to do is ask the questions and then listen with their heart. They should not say anything but the questions, and remind them to refrain from judgment. This is a possibility exercise and needs all the positivity you can create.

Here are a couple examples:

> What do you really want? I want a new winter coat.

> What form do you see it taking? It's dressy and warm, long and black.

> How do you feel? I feel warm, fashionable, and attractive. I feel great.

> What do you really want? I want to vacation in Cancún.

> What form do you see it taking? I want to go in February with a group of friends. We'll stay in a beautiful home that has plenty of room for all of us to spread out, relax, and have a blast together.

> How do you feel? So happy. I feel loved, connected, deserving, and prosperous.

Ten minutes may feel like a long time, but keep going. Say anything that comes to mind. Allow yourself to want, and want, and want some more. When the timer goes off close your eyes and breathe for two minutes. Allow the breath to expand you and create space around all the wanting that you just did.

After two minutes have passed, talk with your partner about what it felt like to want. Was it fun? Was it hard? Did you feel self-conscious about wanting so much? Did you find yourself wondering what the other person was thinking about your wanting? There's so much to discover about your relationship to wanting.

The most important part of this exercise is to realize that the feelings behind your wanting are here, right now. You don't need any "thing" to feel wonderful, prosperous, successful, happy, etc. You can go straight for the feeling, get it activated, and enjoy it. In so doing, the things you desire will come more quickly and easily—because you feel good first.

The next step in ending the suffering game is a big one. It's intentionally placed after you've created a really great foundation with your new God, cleared your consciousness with forgiveness, and started to love yourself enough to put yourself first and to want what you want with no apologies. It's called surrender. It's a simple word you've heard your whole life, but it's a big idea few people really understand.

5

Surrender

There's power in letting go. Take your hands off the wheel and let God drive. He knows the best path for your life.

—Joel Osteen

Twenty years ago I went through a big surrender experience that taught me a lesson I will never forget. I learned that in all things I can trust that God always has my back, even when it doesn't look that way. Let go—and allow God to fulfill your desires. And when you do, they will materialize better then you could have imagined.

It was 1993, and I had just received very clear inspiration that I was to become a minister. I was so happy and certain this was the appointed path for me. I knew the school I wanted to go to and immediately began putting all my effort, time, and money into taking the preliminary classes needed, as well as overloading my schedule with service and leadership requirements. I worked my butt off and loved every minute of it. I had never felt such a clear sense of purpose.

After two years of hard work and a lot of sacrifice, it was finally time to apply. I meticulously filled out the application and gathered up a group of friends to pray with me over it before sending it off. After mailing it I felt such an amazing feeling of accomplishment and joyous anticipation. I knew the two-month waiting period would fly by, I'd receive my letter of acceptance, and then I'd pack up my life in Chicago and move to Kansas City for the next couple years.

When I opened my rejection letter I was devastated. How could this have happened to me? I was confused, lost, and angry. I felt so misguided—foolish, really.

With my dream of being a minister out the window, I threw my belongings in a rental truck and drove across the country. As far as I was concerned, God and I were done. After a few months I started getting settled into a new life, but I couldn't let go of feeling screwed over by God and the anger that accompanied it. In sharing what happened with a friend, he listened intently and at the end said six words: "You should let that story go."

Story?! This isn't a story! This actually happened, I thought to myself. I felt offended and misunderstood, and all my original feelings stirred within me as if I were back in Chicago on that fateful day. Driving home, I noticed a sign at a church displaying the sermon title for the upcoming Sunday. It said, "Do you want to be right or free?" Suddenly, it all started to make sense.

When I got home I went to my bedroom and knelt by my bed. I folded my hands in prayer and began talking to God. I had not done this in quite some time. I told God everything I was feeling. I shared my anger, confusion, and disappointment. In a moment of silence I heard from within me, "Let it go." I was clear at that moment what my problem was—I really wanted to be right—God screwed me over! But I also knew I was suffering and couldn't stand that feeling much longer. So I said, "OK, God, a big part of me doesn't want to do this, but I'm giving this one to you. I'm asking you to help me let this story go and show me how to welcome you back into my heart."

The next Sunday I decided to attend service at Agape International Spiritual Center. There were a thousand people there—it was standing room only. I sat down, sandwiched between two strangers, and closed my eyes as the meditation began. Within the first minute I heard within myself, "You will become a minister here." Tears started streaming down my face as I felt a full surrender of the anger and the sweet relief of true surrender.

Though it took a lot longer and happened in a completely different way than I had planned, looking back, it turned out a hundred times better than anything I ever could have imagined. The program I graduated from stood on the shoulders of all I had previously learned, and the two combined made me triply trained for the calling. I was beyond grateful, because I learned that God did for me what I could not do for myself, and once I surrendered, a higher plan revealed itself. And it was magnificent.

What is surrender? In its deepest sense, it is giving up all the fixing, figuring out, managing, and controlling that keep you bound in chronic fear and confusion. It's letting go of every part of you that thinks it has to make life happen either for yourself or another. It's trusting life so implicitly that you never question it, argue with it, or call it wrong. It's living fully in the moment, with no worry or concern for what will happen next and no expectations on how you or others are supposed to act. You no longer stress about who will or won't show up, what will or won't be said, what will or won't be liked and appreciated. You surrender wanting everyone to be who you think they should be and allow them to be who they truly are. And the coolest part is that this also includes you. *You* become free from all your internal rules and boxes you have created that keep you small and stuck. In surrender you happily relax into being your most fabulous, unpretentious, unpredictable, and unprecedented self. Sounds awesome, right? So why is it so hard to do? And what is it that we're surrendering to?

The Will of God Is Always Good

I call it "the will of God that is *always* good." The will of God can always be trusted but not always understood. It is the light in the darkness and the buoy in the storm. The will of God is that you be happy, free, and living your most amazing life. The will of God is that you never worry about tomorrow, that you live in the certainty that every problem has a right solution, and that solution is here, now. The will of God is that you surrender all that is unlike your glorious perfection so that you may know how loved and precious you truly are.

What dream are you holding too tightly out of fear that it won't come true? Are you in a relationship that isn't working, but the idea of surrendering drums up deep anxiety that you will lose it altogether? Do you have a job that you know is not right for you, but the idea of letting it go creates images of being homeless and hungry? What habits (eating, television, gossip, lying, etc.) are you trapped in to the point that surrender seems impossible?

In God all things are possible! But you've got to let God in. This requires faith. You may not be a pro at turning on the faith and using it in times of need, but that doesn't mean it's not there. You activate your power of faith by calling upon it. Say, "Right here, right now, I call upon my faith to help me let go completely. I call upon my faith to give me the strength to allow life to happen perfectly for me. Dear God, thy will be done."

When you can really trust God (life, source, love, spirit), not just when it appears to be in your favor but at every moment, surrender becomes a really fun and easy thing to do.

Surrender the Who, What, Where, How, and When

Far too often we don't understand where to focus our energy and attention. Because we become nervous and uncertain around whether the universe will provide, and we do not fully believe that God has our back, we begin meddling in areas where our help is not needed. We do not fully let go, which means we stress, struggle, and suffer.

Your job is threefold: Think about what you want. Feel good. Let God do the rest. Remember, this Universe is a yes machine, and it brings your personal God great joy to serve, sustain, and satisfy you. The reason this can be really challenging is because it means you have to surrender the heavy lifting.

As I reflect back upon the days of birthing the Bodhi Spiritual Center, I am in awe of how this Universe made it happen. Often I would look around the room at one of our planning meetings and think, "In a million years I could never have picked this group of people. This is so cool!" I didn't know most of them in the beginning. They came from near and far, drawn by a vision of building something magnificent and new. It was like a magnet was sitting in the middle of the dream effortlessly pulling the right people together.

When it came time to find a place for us to hold our services I could have combed the city, worked all hours, and lost sleep trying to figure it out. Instead, I asked the God of my being to do it for me. I said, "Guide me to the perfect place. I don't have time to waste." Sure enough—within a couple days, with very little effort, I was sitting across from a beautiful woman who owned a metaphysical bookstore in Chicago. She had a large meeting room that she used for lectures and workshops. I knew in my heart this was the place, but I didn't want to become attached, so I checked in with God. "Hey, if this is it, make it clear. This or something better." With that quick check-in I knew I couldn't lose. Let it be, if it's meant to be. I asked the woman who owned the store if it was possible for us to meet there. She paused, looked at me, and said, "I've had more churches come asking to hold services here than I can count. I've always said no. But this time, I'm saying yes."

The right person to create the logo and do the advertising showed up. All we needed, from chairs to a sound system, decorations to invitations, and everything in between came together like magic. I and those who were working with me were having so much fun not *making* things happen but *allowing* them to that one man said, "This is so unbelievable!" Immediately another person countered, "No, it's *so* believable!" We all laughed because we knew it was true. Throughout the entire experience of birthing Bodhi we surrendered the who, what, how, where, and when, and we had the best time doing it.

You cannot make life happen. You allow it to happen. In the midst of fear's stronghold, when you're uncertain if you can let go of your carefully laid plans or the need to make sure something goes the way you think it should, ask, "What else might this vast Universe have in store for me that I haven't even conceived? What could be better than this? What's possible right now if I surrender?" Instead of trying to make things happen your way, and then deflating in disappointment when things don't work out the way you'd imagined them, take a stand for you and your God by saying, "OK, God. I surrender and allow the absolute very best thing possible to occur. Thy will be done."

Control: The Great Illusion

We believe we must control everything and everyone—those we love and those we don't even know. Seriously think about this for a moment. From the time you wake up in the morning, your mind begins talking to you about how you and others should look, act, and think differently. All day long the mind chatters about how this, that, and the other thing is being done incorrectly, won't happen, or will fall apart if you don't control it.

The belief that you have to control life is a pervasive and powerful illusion. What multiplies and sustains this way of thinking is the fact that you have coconspirators in it—basically all of humanity. The game of this world is to pretend we are in charge, and to lose control implies weakness. The truth of how powerless we are over life can feel overwhelming—too much to even contemplate. But we know that deep inside we are vulnerable. We realize our life here on this planet is temporary. But instead of embracing this truth and allowing it to generate present-moment appreciation, we hide out in fear by trying to control that which is uncontrollable. It's goofy and only creates suffering, but we're hooked.

One of our favorite delusional places to focus control is on other people. The moment you find a fault in another, you are trying to change them. If somebody has a quality about them that you do not like, you immediately judge and think they should be different. This may not seem or feel like control to you, but underlying the impulse to correct, improve, point fingers, or outright attack someone is the belief that something is wrong with them and it should be, has to be, *must be* changed (or controlled).

We seldom stop and ask, "Why am I making their 'fault' my problem?" Think about this—if your partner has a short temper, it is *his* problem. If your friend is jealous, it is *her* problem. If your mother decides to continue smoking even though the doctor tells her not to, why do you agonize? If your neighbor decides to paint his house neon pink, even though you could find a thousand people to agree with you that it's hideous, where does that leave you?

The suffering, controlling belief says if only "they" would stop choosing that loser boyfriend, living in nasty places, or wearing that revealing outfit . . . If only "they" would stop being so lazy, put the pizza down, and exercise! . . . If "they" would just stop drinking or using drugs and get clean and sober, finally! . . . If "they" could just see you're only trying to help. . . . *Then* everything would be OK.

You lose your own sense of peace every time you work yourself into a state of worry, despair, or agony over someone else's choices. The reality is nobody changes anything about him- or herself just because someone else thinks they should. Your son, daughter, brother, sister, friend, or foe will not stop doing what they're doing because you see a better way for them. This is true about simple habits and destructive ones alike. And it's true about you and me.

Please note: leaving others alone to be who they are does not negate your responsibility to assist your children or those placed in your care. If it is part of your job to help others make healthy choices and even deter them from making dangerous ones, then it is your responsibility to make sure you personally do so from a place of love and acceptance, with an intention of always up-leveling their sense of personal dignity. Control does not do this—quite the opposite.

Let's also acknowledge that keeping your controlling tendencies in check doesn't mean you're a doormat and you should allow people to walk all over you. Your self-care should never be compromised. It's not always easy to create clear boundaries with loved ones who may be powerless over hurting others or themselves. Life definitely calls us to take courageous steps—ones that make our stomachs flip-flop and our hearts break. I personally know the pain and fear, as well as the triumph, of having to tell a loved one he is not welcome in my home because he is high on drugs and unable to break his addiction. The reason this was empowering for my friend and me was because I was focused on taking care of myself, not on controlling him or wanting him to change. Of course I prayed for his sobriety; but I was very clear I am not in control of that. My love and acceptance of him, exactly as he is, would assist him in finding the help he desired much more quickly than my judgments and condemnation.

Becoming free from control is a two-way street. To the extent I stop trying to control others I also end up being kinder and more accepting of myself. To the extent I can set myself free from my own recrimination, my compassion flows more generously toward others. Working to release control from both vantage points, inward and outward, speeds up the game of letting go and ending the suffering.

Surrender, or Suffer Your Expectations

We also trap people with so many expectations, and sadly, it's often the ones we love the most. We expect them to clean the house the right way, fill the gas tank, do the dishes, wear this and not that, remember important holidays, and anticipate what we want without having to ask. At the same time, we also project upon them negative expectations that they will forget, disappoint, not succeed, and do a half-assed job. We expect all over them and then declare inwardly or outwardly, "I *knew* you would (or wouldn't) (fill in the blank)." When it comes to ourselves, we're even less compassionate. We expect ourselves to do better, not make mistakes, and, God forbid, not embarrass ourselves by looking or acting stupid. We expect ourselves to be polite, remember everyone's name, never have a need that is an imposition to another, and never get angry or upset.

Expectations have big price tags on them. You don't see this in the moment that you are activated by your expectations, but if you pay close attention you will see that they don't feel good. They bring you down and cause you to be disappointed and dissatisfied.

For a few, complete surrender of control and expectations can happen in one moment. People like Eckhart Tolle and Byron Katie are two current examples of people who awakened in an instant and now travel the world helping others experience the effortless joy they live in. For most, surrendering will occur over time and in layers, like peeling an onion. You'll experience a bit of it and feel wonderful and then discover as time goes by that there is another layer to release. No matter the time it takes, surrender is a touchstone on the path to ending your suffering. You will absolutely get there, one step at a time.

Exercise: Place Your Dreams on the Altar of the Holy Spirit

This is a meditative exercise that, with practice, can be done quickly and easily, anytime and in any place.

Close your eyes and take a deep, slow breath. Breathe deeply a couple more times, feeling your body relax. . . . Guide your attention gently into your heart. . . . Once you are there, imagine breathing through your heart for three full inhale and exhale cycles. . . .

When you feel centered in your heart, begin to imagine there is a beautiful altar in the center of it. . . . Allow the image of the altar to become very clear. What is it made out of? Wood? Metal? Stone? Is it rustic or modern? It the altar outdoors or in a room? . . . Take a moment to make this a sacred altar by seeing flowers and perhaps a sacred statue or symbol on it. . . .

See yourself standing in front of the altar and see an image of your personal Divine appear on the other side, opposite you. Do not struggle to imagine what your personal Divine looks like—it can simply be a beautiful, glowing, golden light. . . . Take a moment to feel the unconditional love, acceptance, and support flowing toward you from this beautiful presence.

Now, look down and see around your feet some rocks the size of a baseball. These represent the relationships, dreams, and struggles that are causing you suffering. Reach down, pick up a rock, and bring to mind what or whom it represents. As it becomes clear to you, place the rock on the altar and say to your personal Divine, "I give this to you in full surrender. Please (heal, create, take care of, bring to me) this."

Pick up another rock and do the same thing with something else that you have been holding on to or trying to control. Repeat this several times until you feel relief and a sense of freedom from control, fixing, managing, etc.

Take a deep breath and say ten times, "I surrender. I surrender. I surrender . . . " Give gratitude to your Divine, and as you come back from the meditation, know in your heart that which you have placed on the altar is being taken care of. You can enjoy your day and be about the business of feeling good!

As I said earlier, the more you do this, the easier it will become. You can get to a point where you can just say, "I place this on the altar of the Holy Spirit," and you will feel the relief of surrendering.

Exercise: Inventory Your Expectations

It's important to see how much your life is run by expectations.

Grab your journal or notebook. At the top of the page, write: "Expectations I place upon my family and friends." Then set a timer for thirty minutes. Think of different people, and take note of all that you expect from them. List your expectations without stopping or thinking about it. Write every thought that comes to mind—especially the "crazy ones." Try not to stop or lift the pen from the page. For example:

My partner—I expect him to: Clean the house and do half the chores. Buy me nicer gifts for my birthday and holidays than anyone else. Take care of me when I'm sick. Be faithful. Tell me the truth. Take care of our dogs. Pay the bills. Allow me to be moody and sometimes unkind. Put up with my habits and chronic inability to make the bed. Love me when I'm fat . . .

My mother—I expect her to: Have the holidays at her house. Lend me money when I need it. Criticize me for what I wear. Judge the people I date.

My boss—I expect her to: Not ask me about my personal life. Treat me like I'm her machine and not a person. Give me a raise. See how well I'm doing without me having to point it out.

The list of expectations should fill the pages. You'll discover some you deem "good" and others "bad." This exercise is not about that—it's about seeing how many filters of expectations are in the way of you seeing your loved ones as they truly are, in this very moment.

Once you've completed that list, it's time to do the same for yourself! (Ugh, I know. But this is important work.)

Write at the top of a new piece of paper: "Expectations I place upon myself." Set the timer for twenty minutes, and write, write, and write some more. Here are some examples:

I expect myself to: Be nice. Make more money. Not rock the boat. Weigh what I weighed twenty years ago. Not tell my truth if it might upset someone. Keep my sexual desires a secret. Not be a burden.

After completing this exercise, take a nice long walk or a hot bath. Pamper yourself, because you just got a fast glimpse into the world of expectations that keeps the suffering game activated within you. Please don't make yourself wrong about this. *Everybody has this pile of expectations*—the difference is you were just willing to analyze them, which is what is required for them to begin dissolving. These expectations will have less power over you once you've taken the time to see them.

It's really powerful to share these lists with a trusted friend, therapist, minister, or whoever loves and accepts you. In the 12-step program they call this the fifth step. It's taking the time to let someone else see your underbelly and show you that you are perfectly lovable and not alone.

Sigh! This was a big chapter, huh? I am proud of you. You are more than halfway through, which means you are ready to allow yourself to receive all the blessings that are here for you. Here's the key—you just need to learn how to *really* receive.

6

Generously Receive

Make sure you don't go to the ocean with a teaspoon. At least bring a bucket so the kids won't laugh at you.

—Jim Rohn

I t is said that it is good to give generously. And I agree. In fact, I think it's great to give. But if you don't have a strong and healthy ability to receive, how much do you really have to offer? You can only give to the extent you can receive, so let's get our receiving into top-notch shape.

I once knew a very proud older lady who had to go into the hospital for surgery. Her family and community pitched in to help her recover by bringing her food and taking care of her dog, house, and yard while she was away. She would say over and over, "Oh, you don't have to do that," or, "I'm so sorry to be a burden." She felt so bad about all these people helping her that I actually found myself wondering if accepting the help would make her more sick in the long run.

Long after she had recovered, she would still reference all the help she got. It came from a place of gratitude, but it was always mixed with guilt, as she ended her sentences with, "I just feel so bad that people had to go out of their way." Needing to be helped caused this sweet woman to suffer before her surgery, during her recovery, and long past the healing of her body. She was clearly conditioned to be proud and to suffer if anyone had to go remotely out of their way for her. The irony, which I'm guessing you may relate to, is that this woman would bend over backwards to help somebody else. I believe her desire to give was genuine, but why did she struggle so much with receiving help from others? Why did she feel so bad about it?

We don't let ourselves fully receive because we feel like we don't deserve. Or, we feel obligated and trapped in the receiving. Because we have been taught to feel unworthy we deflect compliments, a helping hand, and the many ways this Universe is offering support. I am certain that the entire suffering game would end altogether if we were better able to generously practice receiving.

I'm not just talking about getting help when you're in trouble, sick, or in dire need. I'm talking about outrageous receiving morning, noon, and night. This is a quantum leap in understanding what receiving is and how it can make your life hum with ease.

We'll need to make some adjustments to get this mindset in place. Just as in all the steps that have come before this one, when it comes to receiving we have been trained to place a lot of rules around it, making it painful, embarrassing, and even shameful to do. Out of the fear of being ridiculed or seen as weak, we've been taught to put huge walls of resistance around ourselves that keep us from allowing and accepting help.

In the old era, being fiercely independent and acting as if you had no needs was widely admired and recognized as healthy. You really were better off going it alone, because being vulnerable and needing help were considered weak, which made you open for attack and ridicule. The old era was about presenting to the world a false image of strength on the outside while crumbling in fear and insecurity on the inside. If you ever did need help, it was practically required that you feel bad about it, shrink down in shame, apologize profusely, and definitely intend to repay whoever came to your rescue. In no uncertain terms were you to accept help for free.

This all comes out of an old belief that says, "Only the strong survive." But remember, that era is dying quickly, and you are here to live in a whole new world. This new era is the very opposite of the old one.

In the new era, being vulnerable and accepting help is smart, honest, and empowering. Honoring your needs and allowing them to be generously met create greater accomplishments and make you feel loved, connected, and cared for. Being fiercely independent will no longer make you well-regarded, but will instead move you out of the game and onto the sidelines of life, alone. Pretending to be confident on the outside while feeling afraid on the inside will no longer be ignored for the sake of saving face. Honest alignment between your inner and outer worlds is not only necessary, it is also celebrated and admired.

The great spiritual teacher Ernest Holmes once said, "You are either attracting or repelling according to your mental attitudes." Your mental attitudes of being worthy or unworthy, happy or unhappy, open or closed, trusting or skeptical are all causing your natural ability to receive, expand, or contract. But you're not a victim to this. You can increase your ability to receive and attract, and in turn more avenues than you could have possibly imagined will present themselves.

Admit It—You Need!

Admitting your need for help, support, love, care, attention, and guidance is the first step in receiving generously. The ego refuses to admit it has needs. When you identify with the ego, you too take this stance. You become defiant and say things like, "I don't need you!" In your fear you push help away by saying, "Forget it. I'll do it on my own." Every time you take a rebellious stance out of fear and false pride, two things happen: (1) You block your receiving; and (2) You suffer.

Here are some more examples of what we say to block life's generous flow. Notice if you have said:

> "I can't find anyone to help me."
> "I'll just do it myself."
> "There's no solution."
> "I know he'll forget to do it."
> "I'm sure she won't remember she said she'd help."
> "I always attract losers."

The list of diminishing phrases we say, unaware of their power to block our ability to see and receive solutions, could go on and on. Solutions, care, and support are always at hand—we just impede our own ability to receive or see them.

In order to receive you must become comfortable with this truth: You need. You need *all day long*. In fact, we all do. It's our nature to need and then have our need fulfilled by receiving. It's a never-ending, beautiful circle of life—need it, receive it, fulfill it, and then start all over again.

I was counseling an extremely talented woman, Maggie, who was really stuck in her music career. Although her voice is amazing, truly God-given, she struggled at every turn. She could not get the breakthrough she wanted. Every time someone came along who had the business connections to move her forward, something would go wrong—she would either not like them, not trust them, or she would sabotage the opportunity in some silly way. Her real problem was that she couldn't receive help. As we were talking, she reflected on her childhood and shared that she had many siblings. Her father had passed away when she was very young, and her mother was poor and too proud to ask for help. Accepting charity was disgraceful to her mother, and having needs was unacceptable. Maggie, being one of the youngest children, learned early on from her mom and her older siblings to despise and repress her needs.

After listening to Maggie's story, I said to her, "What if the only way to succeed is to receive? What if you need lots and lots of help to get where you want to go?"

Her face turned white as a ghost. She took a deep breath and said, "That makes me feel sick to my stomach."

"I know," I said, "but I think all the struggles are not out there in the world but inside you. I believe a part of you has wanted to receive help, attention, and care since you were very little, but you were taught to turn that part off."

My instructions to her were to say over and over: "It is wonderful to have needs. I have them all day long. I love to need. I need. I need. I need."

I told her to admit it a thousand times a day and to let her trusted friends and loved ones know about her needs. To her surprise, they were happy and supportive. She felt herself opening up more and more, and then one day she got a call from a producer in Los Angeles. He wanted to help her record her new CD! Now Maggie's career is taking off in magnificent ways. And the best part is that she will tell you she had no idea it could be this easy and fun!

Exercise: Pause for Insight

Take a moment now and say out loud, "I admit I have needs. I have lots of them. I need people, support, care, and attention, and I love it."

See if you can find a part of you that *doesn't* like this or want it to be true. . . . Breathe into this resistance and go deeper. . . . Where does this resistance to having needs come from? Is it yours? Your parents'? Society's? Take a deeper breath and allow insights to rise up within you. . . . Don't challenge anything that comes to you, just be curious and open. . . .

Take a few moments and journal about how you feel about needing. Also, while journaling ask the God of your being to tell you what could be possible for you if you admitted you have needs.

Release Your Conditions on Receiving

We have the phenomenal ability to fixate on the wrong aspects of a problem, and when it comes to receiving help it's no different. Rather than focusing on *what* we need help with—the key point—our mind becomes preoccupied with outlining who's helping, how, and when. We addressed this in the last chapter, but let's go deeper into this specifically around receiving. When we hinge specific people, places, and exact times to our needs and desires, we are actually blocking our receiving. We tell the Universe, "Yes, I want to receive, but make sure it comes through my husband!" (Or wife, children, boss, etc.)

In my own life I have come to know that every single thing I need or want is immediately available right where I am. What I also know is that I often trap my partner, parents, family, and friends into having to be the ones who give it to me. When this happens the entire world could be singing "Happy Birthday" to me, but if my partner isn't singing, none of it counts. I could receive a thousand yellow roses, but if I had my heart set on receiving a dozen red roses from my friend then all I see is what I didn't get.

Ending suffering means taking full responsibility for all the ways you have trapped people into being your source of recognition, love, or financial security, and in so doing blocked other opportunities from coming about. No person, job, amount of money, or anything of this world is your source. Instead, they are all channels through which the never-ending, always available Source flows.

Yes, we all have channels (job, family, friends, etc.) that we have come to rely upon. But when a channel goes away or becomes something different—you get laid off from your job, your son goes off to college, you grow apart from an old friend—does the supply leave? *No.* This is where we must go back to the source, open ourselves up, and say, "OK, Spirit. Looks like that channel ran dry. Thanks for letting me share in that experience for as long as you did. Now, in what ways will my good come to me that I haven't even thought of yet? What other possibilities are here? Please open up a new channel (or two or three) through which my greater good can flow."

What would happen if you just said yes to generously, abundantly receiving, and you left the who, the how, and the when up to the Universe? There is so much freedom in doing this. It will make you feel nervous in the beginning. You'll feel the emptiness and uncertainty, the pull within to control and make things happen; but if you just breathe and trust, let go and allow, I promise you will be amazed. The Universe will bring to you what you need if you are wide open and willing to look for it. No matter what shape or form your gifts take, the Universe always delivers.

A practice I love to do is randomly say to the Universe, "Please show me I am loved." Then I simply pay attention and look for it. I don't outline how or where the love comes from, and I don't spend one ounce of energy thinking it might not happen. I know it will, and I allow myself to receive it. This sign could be a flower in a window, but I accept it and say, "Ah, that's it." Because this is so simple and there's really nothing at stake, it's a great way to begin building your trust and letting go muscles.

Whenever I am uncertain of where my resources are going to come from, and how they will arrive, I make sure to first center myself in the knowing that this Universe is always conspiring on my behalf. I remind myself that "I believe and am open to receive." Then I consciously open myself to all known and unknown avenues. I affirm, "My heart, mind, and entire being are open to receive in 360 degrees." In my mind, I see myself surrounded by windows and doors, all of them wide open. As I take a deep breath I pull in images, energy, and synchronicities that will manifest what I need and desire. This places me in the center of receiving and tells the Universe that I am allowing it to dictate the who, the how, and the when of my gifts.

Exercise:
Where Are You Blocking Your Abundance?

Where in your life are you making it difficult for the Universe to give you what you need and want? Do you push away compliments? Do you make others guess what you need? Do you wish people would just know what you want so you don't have to ask for it? These are some of the ways you can block your receiving, and they can be changed with intention and practice.

How do you expand your ability to receive? By always saying yes. Every time you say "no, thank you" to someone trying to help you, what you are really saying is, "I can do this alone. I am not open to receive." Whether it comes from a place of fierce independence, false pride, or you just don't think you need help, every time you decline an offering of assistance, especially in small ways, you are telling the Universe to back off.

If you want to open yourself to receiving, begin right now by never saying no to any offer of help. If someone offers to get the door for you, say, "Why, thank you so much." If someone offers to carry your groceries to the car, say, "Absolutely, I welcome the help." If a friend offers to buy you lunch, instead of the old reply, "Oh, you don't have to do that," your new response is, "Oh, thank you so much! I'm honored and grateful."

Receive, receive, and receive some more. Say to the Universe when you wake up and all throughout the day,

"Universe, bring me more good—and help me to believe it and receive it!"

Affirmation:
The Universe Will Meet Your Every Need

Begin each day with a declaration that this Universe is here for you and will meet your every need. Then stand tall, legs spread and arms reaching high and wide into the sky, and close your eyes. Feel the openness of your whole body and take three deep, fulfilling breaths. With each exhale, imagine yourself receiving, accepting, and opening to your greater good. Allow yourself to slow down a bit as you move through your day, imagining and welcoming guidance and support at every moment.

Exercise: Practice Asking for Help

Take a moment and get really clear about what you need, and then either ask someone directly for help or ask the Universe at large to help you. Be direct as you ask for what you want; don't be vague or passive or apologetic. If the person you ask says no, thank them and honor them, knowing that they are simply making room for the right person to come along.

Pay attention to any feelings of attachment to the who, the where, or the when. If you really want help to come from a certain someone, if you find it scary to articulate your needs, notice these things. This is a hard one, but you can do it. And it will make a *huge* difference, I promise.

Remember, to receive is to allow this Universe to love and support you, and you are more than worth it. Throw open the doors and windows of your mind and heart and allow yourself to receive! Imagine life being easy and magical—because it is!

Receiving is one side of the coin; giving from the overflow is the other. Let's get that side flowing now so you can really experience the balance and perfection of being an inlet and outlet for life.

7

Give Yourself Away

A generous heart, kind speech and a life of service and compassion are the things that renew humanity.

—The Buddha

I believe we have come to this world to master unconditional love for ourselves—to see ourselves as one with God and to completely accept all that we are and are not. Once that is in place, we can find and fulfill the real reason we are here, which is to fully and freely give ourselves away. In this new era we must extend ourselves beyond our body, home, family, and friends. We must grow to see that every person is the beloved, an expression of God, and it is our duty to help others in any way we can. When we have the opportunity to remove the suffering of another, we must do it.

Rumi, the thirteenth-century mystic, said, "When you do things from your soul, you feel a river moving in you, a joy." This river is the life of God. God did not hold back when He/She/It exploded into multiple, countless dimensions of reality. From all the magnificent colors to the many glorious flavors, from the soft and sensual to the hard and majestic, God, as life, gave and will give fully and freely forevermore. You, being one with God, can and will only know yourself as this power when you too do what God does—give yourself away. From the simplest acts of quiet kindness to the dramatic gestures that save lives, and everything in between, we feel alive when we make someone else's life better.

Often we think the need is so extreme that we cannot possibly make a dent in the problem. We sit on the sidelines, drinking our coffee and saying, "What can I do? I'm only one person." To further the apathy, in our society more attention is often given to large, sweeping acts of heroism and generosity, such as going to Africa to build schools or to parts of the world where catastrophic events have devastated the people of that land. Of course this is spectacular work, and I pray there be more and more of this kind of caring and sharing. But I also believe the simple act of making one person's life better, especially if nobody ever sees or notices, is just as beautiful and important.

Seldom do we get a glimpse of the impact our simple actions have on others. Seemingly insignificant moments, when acted upon out of love, can affect history and even change the course of humanity. If you could rise up high above your lifetime, so far that you were able to see the span of your existence and the influence it has upon all creation, you would be dumbfounded to see how your unassuming, generous acts travel out into all of existence as a pure vibration of love. You would know without a doubt that every good deed you do is important. Every loving action generates a ripple upon the waters of creation that joins other ripples that multiply and extend in ways we cannot conceive.

Mitchell Marcus was a student at Coronado High School in El Paso, Texas. He was also the team manager for the Coronado Thunderbirds basketball team. During the last game of the season, with ninety seconds left in the game, Mitchell, who has a developmental disability, was given the opportunity of his lifetime. He was told by his coach to put on his jersey and get on the court and play.

The team passed the ball to Mitchell at every turn, but each time they did Mitchell missed the shot. The entire crowd was chanting, "Mitchell, Mitchell!" The ball went out of bounds and the opposing team took control of the ball. With only seconds remaining, everyone in the crowd knew Mitchell had lost his chance to score.

Then, Jonathon Montanez, a member of the opposing team, tossed Mitchell the ball. Mitchell turned toward the basket, aimed, and scored! The crowd went wild as they jumped to their feet and ran down onto the court to raise and praise Mitchell. Mitchell's mother, Amy, said, "I'll cry about it for the rest of my life." It was an act of kindness, a moment where Jonathon Montanez followed his heart and did something simple that made all the difference in the world.

Sat Karma

Karma is an Eastern word that loosely means the law of cause and effect. Put simply, it's the idea that what you put out into the world returns to you. If you are kind, you will receive kindness. If you are mean and stingy, you will experience the world as such. Sat karma is the intentional practice of making other people's lives better in service to both their liberation and your own. If you committed to practicing sat karma you would, in a very short time, experience greater meaning and deep joy.

There are three types of sat karma: physical, psychological, and spiritual.

Physical Sat Karma

Physical sat karma is when you help others through your words and actions. Many times, consciously or unconsciously, we tend to use words that cause others pain. Right words are words that do not minimize or hurt others. Sometimes you may have good intentions, but your words are perceived by the other person as being harsh. A good intent must be matched by the right words. Words must be sweet, and they must soothe the soul and create gladness. A kind word spoken at the right time can be of immense help to someone who is feeling sad or depressed.

Right actions, like right words, are actions that are sacred and help others in the simplest ways. Opening a door for someone carrying grocery bags or giving a car the right of way while driving are generous acts that extend care and ricochet back to you loads of goodness. They make others feel better. And in so doing, they calm your heart, ease your journey, and build for you a karmic account of invisible and visible support.

Psychological Sat Karma

Psychological sat karma is earned by right thoughts and emotions. You may say, "I'm not doing any harm when I think a negative thought about somebody else. My thoughts are my own." This actually is not true. The negative thought is about another, but it's happening in your mind and your body, and therefore you suffer the effect. Also, every thought you have is energy in motion. It extends to and without a doubt affects those around you. The realm of thought is powerful and creative. Hence, having right thoughts is very important.

Many times you don't want to think negatively, but you are nevertheless plagued by negative thoughts and emotions. This is challenging, but not insurmountable—especially for someone like you, who has come so far in mastering the art of surrender. The right practice is to be intensely aware of your thoughts and emotions without attempting to control or be swayed by them. Become the observer, and in so doing invite the presence of your personal Divine to take away the negative thoughts and assist you in replacing them with positive and productive ones. You don't have to do this alone. You can ask for help. And ask and ask again.

Your willingness to think positively goes a very long way in releasing you from the suffering that habitual negative thinking brings to you and others. You can change your thinking. It often takes time, but you can do it. And you will literally see the results of changing your thinking in the sudden smiles of strangers walking by, in the familiarity you feel with others wherever you are, and in the lightness you feel in your body and mind.

Spiritual Sat Karma

Spiritual sat karma is about helping others to grow spiritually. Doing spiritual practices, praying for others, meditating on world peace, serving in your church or spiritual community, chanting mantras, and joining meditation circles are all examples of ways you can earn spiritual sat karma. Our spiritual sat karma helps us to progress on the spiritual plane. It opens the doors of grace for us and ultimately also leads us to enlightenment.

The More You Give, the More You Have

The greatest gift in giving is the revelation that few get: The more you give, the more you have and the less you need. You learn that joy is not in having or hoarding, but in being the vessel through which so much life energy flows. You become free from a large vibration of suffering by having one of the biggest lies operating in humanity dissolved: the belief that there is not enough. What you have will become enough, and still you will prosper and have more. Feelings of scarcity will become a thing of the past.

You've come much too far to believe the lies of the ego. The truth is that you have so much to give, and when you start sharing your gifts with others, no matter how small the offering, you will see that what you contribute expands into more. You will feel connected, alive, and a deep sense of purpose. At the end of the day, you will lay your head down to sleep with satisfaction that no amount of money or recognition could ever bring.

A few weeks after teaching a class on sat karma, one of my students sent me the following note, which so beautifully depicts the rewards of this work.

I want you to know that your teaching about sat karma is so accurate. There are no better life moments, for me, than when I am in the act of making someone's life more beautiful. There is no delay in gratification, no delay in my own sense of connectedness, of union, of oneness. Thank you so much for that powerful insight as a guiding and pulling force toward enlightenment.

How many billions of people over the centuries have read, heard, spoken, and memorized this quote?

You are the light of the world.

—Matthew 5:14

And yet, how many of those billions of people have still not allowed themselves to *be* the light? What might this world be like today if those countless people had taken this truth into their hearts and hands? How many wars could have been avoided? How many illnesses could have been cured sooner? How much genocide might have been prevented? How much life would have been cherished instead of wasted?

What if you decided to be that light? What would be possible for the world around you? Truthfully, I don't have an answer, simply because there's no limit to what you can do. What I know is that when that light is allowed to have its way with you, mountains move, hearts burst open, resources flood in, and your capacity to care and share grows exponentially.

You will become one of the people who no longer uses your precious energy to complain and point fingers, but to do good. Whether you're simply opening the door for someone or are dedicated to helping lift another out of poverty, you will see love in this person's eyes, and oneness will awaken within your heart and mind. In this state of connectivity, suffering is absolutely impossible.

Exercise: Sat Karma—A Way of Life

I invite you to include in your morning spiritual practice a declaration of who you are here to be and how you intend to make the world a better place today. I like to repeat mine three times: one for my mind; one for my heart; and one for my gut, or feeling nature.

> Today I commit to helping anyone who crosses my path, knowing that we are together for that moment in time for a divine purpose. I think loving thoughts and send blessings to all those around me. I help wherever and however I can. And I consciously behold all people as possible, prosperous, and perfect, just as they are.

This is a simple, powerful, and empowering affirmation that sets me on a path of service each day. If at any point I want to change it, I do. It's fun to allow it to expand into different variations on the theme.

Give Away 10 Percent of Your Time and Watch It Expand

Tithing is an ancient spiritual practice of giving a portion of your income to that which spiritually feeds you. I love to tithe my money and reap the benefits—peace of mind and the practice of remembering God is my source. But tithing isn't only about money. Giving 10 percent of your time and talent is another form of tithing—and just as important and fulfilling.

Let's figure out how many free-time hours you have in a week. Working backwards and calculating how many hours are spoken for already best accomplishes this. Every one of us has 168 hours in a week to work with. Here's an example:

Sleep (8 hours per night x 7 nights per week) = 56 hours

Work (8 hours per day, plus 1 hour commuting each way x 5 days per week) = 50 hours

Self-care (showering, exercising) = 8 hours

Chores (cooking, shopping, cleaning, looking after the kids, etc.) = 25 hours

Spiritual nourishment (church, meditation, classes, etc.) = 10 hours

Miscellaneous = 2 hours

Total = 151 hours

168–151 = 17 hours per week for you to play, relax, and do whatever you desire.

Give 10 percent of that away each week = 1.7 hours of sacred
service.

To me this is very manageable, and it makes a difference to those you serve. It also will make your time expand.
I can't explain how, but I personally know it works, and
you'll know it for yourself too—only by doing it.

Where do you give your time and talent? Well, what
moves your heart? What do you love? If you love animals,
then go to your local animal shelter. Definitely serve at
your spiritual center or church. Sharing your gifts and
talents with your spiritual community, as far as I'm concerned, is a must. Helping your spiritual brothers and sis-
ters awaken to their inner power and truth will absolutely
expand your heart.

You have enormous power within that you can share
with the world around you. You have the right heart that,
when allowed to lead, will give you the words to say that
will help another have hope. You have the exact skills
that are the perfect solution for another's problem. You
are always exactly where you need to be, at the appointed
time, to give yourself away. And in so doing, you will be
the revealer of God's grace. This grace will multiply a
hundredfold and return to you as a feeling of fulfillment
and joy that is priceless.

Conclusion

Congratulations! You've completed an amazing journey, all in the name of taking responsibility for your life and your happiness. You've looked into yourself and your past and discovered that every part of you that suffers can be transformed.

We've moved some pretty big mountains out of the way in the course of this book, but don't be surprised to find there are still more ahead. Our Universe is a magnificent school, one where you are always being guided to your next lesson. Remember, life is proactive, and for you, it is always guiding you along, providing the tools you need to succeed exactly when you need them.

As you continue your journey, practice working *with* life instead of against it. When you do fall or feel like you're starting over (and you will—we all do), don't diminish how far you've come. Instead, take some time each day to reflect and celebrate the littlest of wins. Place your focus on the progress you've made up to this point. This will make small stumbling blocks much easier to overcome. Whenever you are frustrated, sad, or feeling like you can't stay the course, that is the perfect time to do one of the exercises designed to help you remember and realign.

Today my life is so much better than I could ever have imagined. I feel alive, connected, and capable of handling whatever comes. I deeply believe in and experience God in a personal and fulfilling way. I don't need to prove or justify this connection—I just get to enjoy it and allow it to lead me to greater and greater integrity and freedom. When I get hit with a little (or a lot) of shame around what I think, desire, feel, and want, I no longer hide and pretend it's not there. I share it with friends who I know love me and believe in me. This dissolves my insecurity and brings me back into the present moment.

My inner foundation, once cracked, is now more solid than ever. I'm genuinely interested in who I am being and what is occurring inside and around me. I also find it so much easier to say, "Hey, I'm sorry. I made a mistake." Most important of all, I trust life. I'm less concerned with tomorrow or what others are thinking about me. I get that everyone is having his or her own experience, and what others think about me is really none of my business.

This doesn't mean I'm immune to feelings of sadness, anger, frustration, confusion, or disappointment. Life is difficult. It is complex, dynamic, confusing, inspiring, exhilarating, gratifying, miraculous, and enduring. I still feel the full spectrum of emotions, but I don't name these feelings as wrong anymore. I don't try to push them away, suppress them, or hide them from those around me. I am able to fully experience these feelings, which is what ultimately leads to freedom from suffering. "Bad" things will still happen. You will lose that job if it is time to let it go. Your lover will leave if the relationship is over. You may become ill, sometimes with no apparent rhyme or reason.

Will you ever feel disconnected from God? Unquestionably. Will you find it nearly impossible at times to forgive because you're so committed to being right? Absolutely. Will you stumble at loving yourself? Of course. Will you judge what you want and feel embarrassed about it? Probably. Will you forget to let go and find yourself crazily trying to control? Sure. Will you push away the support of others out of a false sense of pride? Heck yeah! Will you forget to help make somebody's life easier? Yes, you will.

What is different is who you are in relationship to these things happening. I want you to look forward to the next time you feel suffering. (*Whaaaat?*) Stay with me here—this is good news. Now you have the tools to deal with your life. Today is the day you no longer have to run from suffering or end up wallowing in it like a victim. Now, suffering is your friend, your guidepost that says, "Hey, pay attention. Something's off here and you need to stop and look at it."

Progress, Not Perfection

Changing your thought patterns and behaviors takes time. One of my favorite quotes from the Big Book of Alcoholics Anonymous is, "You will be amazed before you are halfway through." This is a promise given to people who are taking their first steps toward doing what they need to do to get sober. Once they have surrendered and are open to learn, they move into an unknown world with very little understanding of how to navigate it. But by making one choice for freedom at a time, and opening themselves to accepting support from others, many find their way out of extreme suffering and into a much better, brighter world.

You are offered this same promise. God, the grace that is beyond all human understanding, will rise up and support you and carry you if need be—always and forever more.

Acknowledgments

It is with a full and grateful heart that I thank the Bodhi spiritual community for all their love and support. I really appreciate who we have become. We have grown up together. Not always easy—but deeply inspiring and worth it.

To my publisher, Randy Davila. I thank you for your support and commitment to helping me go deeper. To Allison and Susie who also helped in refining this book. I'm grateful for your time and expertise.

And to every person along my path who has helped me surrender, start over, laugh, cry, scream, or just be . . . thank you.

About the Author

Rev. Mark Anthony Lord is an internationally recognized author, speaker, and teacher and the senior minister of the Bodhi Spiritual Center—a community that is here to broadcast love! He founded this spiritual center in November 2003 in the back of a metaphysical bookstore in Chicago. Since its humble inception, it has grown into a flourishing community where thousands of people seek out Mark Anthony's wisdom each week by attending Sunday services or weekly classes, or by listening to his podcasts.

He is a gifted communicator who uses humor, current events, and personal stories to help his students ask deep questions that allow genuine transformation. His personal mission is to assist people in awakening to the healing power of self-love, acceptance, and a more expanded, deeply personal God that is greater than any problem. He is a master at translating ancient sacred teachings into accessible language, and his messages are inspiring and practical.

A passionate, lifelong learner, Mark Anthony received his training at Unity, Agape International Spiritual Center, Science of Mind, and Oneness University in India. He is also the author of *The Seven Living Words: An Illuminated Perspective on the Seven Last Words of Jesus*.

He is most proud of his deep knowing that being gay is a gift not just for himself but the world, and he is grateful for seventeen years with his husband Patrick and their loving family.

Hierophant publishing
books that inspire your body, mind, and spirit

Hierophant Publishing
8301 Broadway, Suite 219
San Antonio, TX 78209
888-800-4240

www.hierophantpublishing.com

Made in the USA
Middletown, DE
27 June 2021